結 構 與 歷 史

略談中國古經文的組成問題

Structure and History

Remarks on Problems
in the Composition of
Ancient Chinese Classical

Texts

Scott Davis

戴 思 克 著

文史哲出版社印行

The Liberal Arts Press

國家圖書館出版品預行編目資料

結構與歷史：略談中國古經文的組成問題=
Structure and History：Remarks on Problems
in the Composition of Ancient Chinese
Classical Texts / 戴思克（Scott Davis）著.
-- 初版 -- 台北市：文史哲, 民 84.05
　面；　公分
ISBN 978-957-547-951-0（平裝）

1.歷史—哲學，原理

601.4　　　　　　　　　　　　　84004193

結構與歷史
略談中國古經文的組成問題
Structure and History
Remarks on Problems
in the Composition of
Ancient Chinese Classical
Texts

著　　者：戴　思　克　Scott Ddavis
出 版 者：文　史　哲　出　版　社
　　　　　http://www.lapen.com.tw
　　　　　e-mail：lapen@ms74.hinet.net
登記證字號：行政院新聞局版臺業字五三三七號
發 行 人：彭　　　正　　　雄
發 行 所：文　史　哲　出　版　社
印 刷 者：文　史　哲　出　版　社
　　　　　臺北市羅斯福路一段七十二巷四號
　　　　　郵政劃撥帳號：一六一八○一七五
　　　　　電話886-2-23511028・傳真886-2-23965656
定價新臺幣一六○元
一九九五年（民八十四）五月初版

ISBN 978-957-547-951-0　　　61013

結 構 與 歷 史

略談中國古經文的組成問題

目 次

不管外在世界物質性特質如何，必須有人類才有天地。「天地」，我們的宇宙，則是包涵在人類界線中的客觀物體界，心理世界，以及人間文化座標。外在物質的空間是有它本身的時間，可是有天地才有歷史。斷定歷史的特點基於它的敘述特質。有構成敘述的條件才可能產生含有意義的事件。

　　那麼，意義，劇情，角色，主題，焦點等等的敘述特質，怎麼會在外在世界形成的呢？這個問題在西方哲學史已經獲得種種的答案；大體上像讀者觀感理論裡的，強調敘述效果是由閱讀者對於文章形式上的組織而反應的。這種理論傾向於哲學的唯心論，而有太誇張主觀因素的危險。另外，想要解釋敘述效果為客觀存在品質的理論則得面對說明這種外在獨立存在情況的困處。因此最合理的方向應該是採取相互作用的理論。敘述特質就是繼承人類的行動和認識才產生真實外在的品質。換一句話而言，這些特質是包含於人類的文化媒體而演變出來的。

　　如康德所論證的，在人類經驗中，時間跟空間是必有的空框。因此，時間也必須有空間化的可能。斷定歷史的敘述特質，基於時間分為開始，中間，和結尾三段。歷史現出的意義是基於開始與中間階段的價值能夠依靠結尾的價值而定的。我們常常發覺，歷史上所敘述的事件，知道了其後果才能瞭解其開頭，結尾會在中間階段來調整它開頭的意義。因而中間部份可能成為前後的轉軸。這種三個階段的構造是和物質性因果關係迥然不同。就因爲因果關係的概念缺乏媒介的問題，所以羅素[1] 到最後便提出因果關係是任何具有功能形式定律的說法。只有在人間維持的天地，才有這種三個階段的敘述特質。而且，這種時間異於因果關係的，不是專從前到後，早到晚，單向而流。反而，目前與過去事件的意義也可能依靠未來而定的。

在中國古代經文當中也不例外。如果從它敘述性的特點來針對它的組織，我們會發覺古代中國經文的設計是基於這種特性。這方面的問題，由於考證學的長久壟斷漢學，所以比較不受重視。我在這篇文章所要探討的是古經文結構安排的分析。我會舉幾個例子加以討論；雖然疑問比答案多，但或許可以促進學術界恢復一點對於古經文整體上組織結構的興趣。

數理科學

先來考慮數目字吧。在邏輯上，數目只是一組一組維持逐步次序，而局部則爲互相包涵以及被包涵的集合；在妥當劃分定義工作之下，這些集合就能夠組織外在物體的數量關係。同時乘著各組集合當中內在關係而定的各種操作規則，亦能加以發揮。可是古代中國對數字觀點有別的目標。古代中國數目字最重要的用意是爲了體現宇宙整體。因此，這類的傳統異於典型早期數學的運用，如加減，計帳，量數…等等。古代中國數學傳統較重視把所象徵的宇宙整體，除分爲各種屬組。在那種操作系統裡，有計量數與序數分別不明顯的趨勢。主要的問題不是數量的多少，而是各屬組怎麼分別出來，以及在整體之內置於何位。略如現代拓撲學一樣，古代中國數學不以數量為主而是以整體各處形勢分配為主。

　　舉例而言：在中國古代「一」到「十」，這些基本的整數。「九」常常是象徵宇宙各方面的整體，譬如「九方」就代表全世界。可是「九」也是「十」：因為當整體的「九」也能算為「一」，九方和它整體合起來等於十。這種方程式，在傳統中國思想裡是常常遇到的。同時，「一」到「十」得反映各種宇宙觀方面的功能。在它中間的「五」，古字體正像個叉叉（X）顯示得很清楚它轉扭的作用。「五」和「六」即為承上轉下的中心，而它們總數為十一；中心上下的其他數目，同樣的配合而為十一：如四加七，三加八，二加九。這是眾所周知河圖洛書裡的基本知識。因此，傳統中國數學離不開這種魔術方塊的概念。

日曆性的時間

　　二來考慮天干地支。以十個符號配合十二個符號來做時間的記錄，已經顯然是把時間的流向加以結構化。更值得注意的是：這不只是抽象形式上的符號，而是曾經帶過意義的象徵。這個制度運用在古代宇宙觀的前題下，因之顯示出當時宇宙觀的肌理與輪廓。以天干來講，「甲」的象徵性，難免讓人連想開放，發出，生長等等的宇宙功能。而「乙」則有返回之意，略如乾坤的對稱意義。在地支上，「子」在最開頭也是一種不禁令人推敲的資料[2]。而在中間位置相當於十二屬相中「蛇」的「己」與「巳

3

」，都是在第六位置。這些字形的本身已具有扭曲與承上轉下的特徵。（「已」與「巳」不都似蛇行之狀？）

　　還有，不能不問，在天干地支第四位的「丁」與「卯」的被遺忘的意義。「丁」寫成一點，而「卯」則是分開的兩半。「卯」是指一種犧牲儀式[3]。而在商朝這種重視「四」的數目的宇宙觀（四方，四季等等），第四位應該有它的特色（譬如四方之中算不算一個單獨的位置等等的問題）。「丁」跟「卯」配合在一起應該含有這類「一分爲二，二合爲一」的涵意，因爲「丁」是一整體的一點，而「卯」是分開爲二的。**它們應該是在同樣的背景之下連在一起的。**總而言之，天干地支除了是一個數學性的工具之外，也具有神話性。而在它象徵網絡當中所衍發的關係，也還能演變出它敘述性的宇宙觀。

理想的政體

　　政府的功能有沒有這種秩序呢？誰都認爲**周禮**是一本曾經經過大量的，徹底的設計；可是很少有人考查它結構上的安排。有趣的是，**周禮**內連最瑣碎的事務，也可能顯示出古中國的宇宙分類的範疇或座標。比方說，**周禮**裡的「王」要吃甚麼？〈天官〉描寫出一整套陣容，都爲了讓王能夠吃飽。一共有十個位置，如下：膳夫，庖夫，內饔，外饔，亨人，甸師，獸人，漁人，鱉人，臘人。從各方面來看，這個單子具有很嚴格的形式結構。很明顯的，這十個位置分爲上下兩半。頭兩對都是比較位於內的；

4

兩個「夫」是接近火的，做烹飪的。之後，有兩個辦「饗」的，也是從內到外。最後四個，都是某「人」的，而都是負責供獻各種獵獸食物；因此是比上一半更向野外的，更「自然」的。這四個單位當中也具有個很仔細的組織。他們其實也是一對一對的；他們的範圍跟重要性是越來越小。陸上的獸相對於水中的魚，正像從水中來的小「互物」（蚌殼，烏龜，等等）相對於被晒乾或烤過的腊肉。這四個單位中最後的「腊人」的事就提到其中最前面的獸人所提供的；其實，腊肉是依靠獵獸的肉。「獸人」的責任是在冬天的時候要提供狼，在夏天就提供一種鹿，而在「春秋」的時候提供「獸物」。這就是說，夏天和冬天都分得很清楚，而春秋的季節卻分不清楚，當兩季所獵的動物也分不清楚。反而，「漁人」的工作指定在春天，而「鱉人」是春天提供鱉與蜃，秋天提供龜與魚。「腊人」是靠「獸人」，則無定時。可見，安排這單子的人，當時就很費心的思考。

中間兩個位置是比較特別的。「甸師」是在其中唯一的叫作某「師」的，而也是唯一的從事提供農業產品的。「亨人」具有扭轉的功能；雖然他在前一半，可是他還像下一半的一樣叫某「人」。再說，他跟甸師都有對於火和水的責任。尤其是「亨人」特別指出他跟「水火」的關係。這個陣容有十個單位，而在其中間出現「水火」字，並不是隨機的。當時，要服務天子生活的人，絕對不是隨便設想的，而是具有代表整體宇宙的象徵性；各個在其適當的階級都如此參加了當時的宇宙。

聖人的思考

到目前，所討論的題目都很容易想像有結構性因素的關連。關於數目，時間與政府的符號當然會牽涉到形式上的考慮。那麼，現在我們來探討另外種類的現象。像作爲聖人指示的論語之類的記載，會不會同樣構成結構性的組織？這個問題是針對古經文的整體設計。我們來分析幾個例子之前，先來想應該怎麼替這個學術範圍取名字。在阿里斯多德的基本教育上有三種學問：除了文法和邏輯以外，還有一種教人怎麼辯論的，現代中文翻譯爲「修辭學」，或翻譯「說得術」較妥當一點。目前文學對這方面的問題，已經不限於說服對象的技術，而是用來指各方面敘述性的設計。對我們目前的問題而講，可以說：在表面上，**論語是一篇一篇構成的。可是，像某些人曾寫過**(4)，也許它的次序有關連的意義在。這是容得下一些假設與推想的。對於論語文中的安排問題，本文無從仔細處理，而只能提出幾個線索。

論語篇章安排的次序其實不像完全是隨機的。比方說：第十四篇，第二十七章與二十八章很明顯的有共同意義和字彙：「不在其位，不謀其政」與「君子思不出其位」。因爲前一章是重復第八篇第十四章，所以這類的安排大概是編者在編書的時候連想的。

另外，論語第八篇，第三章至第七章，這五章都關於「曾子有疾」而過世的。如果是隨機安排的話，爲甚麼這些相關的文章會如此連在一起呢？這種現象大概不是後來編書的時候的事，而是本來就有這幾章連在一起的。

　　這類的情形，在論語裡有很多例子。例如，第十三篇，第八和第九章，雖然用意稍微不同，可是兩章都關於「富」的問題，而兩章都把「富」字排在系列的第三位。可見，論語的敘述性效果這問題不是完全沒有根據的。這樣看，想要研究這方面的假設，就非得採用一種基於分布現象的方法不可。

　　再說，論語還有一種敘述性的特質。在裡面出現的人物，常會演出類似一致的角色。顏回，子路等弟子都具有他們固定的角色。樊遲也是一個很明顯的例子。跟他有關的論點包括：祭祀，死，葬，鬼神，「舞雩」，農業，生育，等等比較含有具體生理或宗教意味。因此，當樊遲問到仁跟知的時候（第六篇第二十章），而被回答關於鬼神，以後下一章所講的「知者樂水，仁者樂山」一句，也應該繼續連起來。這樣想來，樊遲這個人物具有一點古代崇拜大自然宗教的意味。

歷史的結構

　　這類的線索很多。目前我們無法達到合適的結論；我們只能以指出問題的存在為目標而已。聖人講的話的記載也可能按照這種形式上的安排而收集。不過，歷史卻不一定同樣。在時間的流向所發生的事情，應該是很典型的偶然的履歷，所以紀錄它的歷史也照理說應該沒有甚麼本身的結構。然而，我們如果看左傳的話，就會開始對此說法懷疑。

　　講到這點，首先必須表明清楚，現在這個題目並不是左傳裡的歷史

7

記載是否準確。要調查歷史資料是不是真的相當於當時所發生的事實，應該在完全另外的一個平面上發展。我們知道，當時中國幾乎每個小國諸侯，都有一部門的人專門做史，來記下重要的事故。目前這個問題不關於這些資料跟外界的連繫，而是要探討左傳本身內在的組織。不管這些故事是從哪兒來的，我們得問道，為甚麼被選為出現在某一年的歷史的資料，就是這些事情，而不是別的呢。我們如果想一想，就會發覺左傳裡有很多地方，假如看為純粹的歷史的話，就很不容易瞭解。就是因為它自號為歷史，所以它的內在組織這個問題，便是那麼的明顯。

左傳為了敘述春秋的歷史所採取的方法，已經是獲得了公共的肯定。尤其是左傳敘述戰爭是特別出名，甚至於最引人注目的文章是關於春秋時代的戰爭。並且，左傳很清楚的傳達當時社會的日常摩擦，演變以及內在結構衝突。讀左傳的讀者，無不欣賞此書尖銳的描寫各人個性以及態度上，是在歷史上佔多麼大的角色。左傳裡的故事常以非常微妙的細節來表章各人的心態，或者是一件事故的最初動態，從未來後果著想的話，能夠顯出多麼重要。而且，將來的事件可能影響目前的事勢。比方說，〈文，六年〉，秦穆公的喪禮用人來殉葬，所以，「君子曰：秦穆之不為盟主也宜哉」。這就是以後來的事情來說明較早的情況了。因此，左傳充滿了這種隆重的帶著「命」的意義的氣氛。誰願意從頭到尾整體來研讀左傳，而不是只斷章截篇，就可以享受到歷史敘述的巧妙交織，前後上下層層遙相呼應互動，而且感覺到古代中國的層次深厚的對於時間的體會。

這些精彩的敘述效果是基於較常見的歷史學特質。除了這些普遍人間的敘述性時間，動機，發展等等之外，左傳也牽涉到另一種結構性的問題，就譬如它常有的平行組織。比方，〈文，十一年〉，在同一年短短的傳文，就提出兩次，「埋其首於…之門」這類的敘述。當然，第二次提的是以左傳出名的「追敘法」，來回顧過去的背景（「初宋武公之世」…）　，而準備發揮後來〈襄，三十年〉的事件；可是從它敘述特質來說，一定有甚麼特定動機選出這個內容來置於此處。然而，這年的傳文錯誤頗多。如果非要勉強的做假設的話，就可以說：我們確知別的地方，重復的文字是錯誤；比方，春秋經在〈襄，二十一年以及二十四年〉都寫了兩次「日有食之」的記錄，肯定一年中沒那麼多日蝕，可見其中一定有一些衍文。也許，「埋其首於…之門」這種重復的辭也就算是編傳文時候的意外了。

再考慮左傳平行組織一次的話，就必須放棄這類的假設。許多例子有重復的內容。譬如，〈成，十三年〉，明顯的具有兩次如下的綱要：（一）某人負責進行某種禮；（二）「不敬」；（三）另外某人教訓關於禮（「禮身之幹也」）或敬（「勤禮莫如致敬」）；（四）而用「惰。棄君〔其〕命也〔矣〕」這些辭句，以做結論。不知道是不是應該說，紀元前五七八年，人人都在談同樣構造的話（當然有可能），或者說，左丘明先生編纂〈成，十三年〉的時候，想要使這年顯出跟這些問題的關連吧。

因為這種例子那麼多，就不用一個一個提出來。我們只以最後一個例子，來開始探討為甚麼某一種平行構造，可能會「屬於」某一年的傳文。〈昭，二十年〉就是紀元前五二二年，也就是說，是從孔丘誕生後的第三十年的時候。這年的資料很豐富；其中有晏子談「和與同異乎」的話題

9

。晏子回答這個問題的時候，就跟烹飪扯上關係，因此自然就提起「水火」的因素來解釋。其實，火水相濟，這方面的比喻在這段是很重要的因素，因為它的結論就包括「若以水濟水，誰能食之」的辭句。緊接著，齊侯就問起「古而無死」的事。奇怪的是：下一場故事是子產死之前最後講的話。而他也討論火跟水這個論點。然後，孔子就繼續發揮前面關於「和」的想法。為甚麼〈昭，二十年〉會那麼主張火和水的象徵呢？

　　這類的證據應該讓我們提高對古代歷史中的結構性組織的警戒。可是，這個問題的範圍不只限於一年一年當中的安排，除了這種微觀規模之外，也不應該忽略宏觀上整體組織的體象。除了是一段歷史之外，它也是具有整體結構的宇宙觀。左傳毫無疑意有設定三個特別的部位：就是開始，中間和結尾。每個部位都給我們一些線索，讓我們注意左傳的儀式文化背景。〈閔公初年〉不可否認從最開始的故事就很明顯的建構了這種儀式意境。鄭莊公與他母親姜氏的糾紛，分離而復合，雖然表面上不一定有更深一層的意義在，可是套上此故事的大前題以及導引－－就是「不及黃泉無相見也」的誓語，「闕地及泉」的妙法，以及「大隧之中，其樂也融融…大隧之外，其樂也泄泄」的公式性行為與言語－－而且顧及它在左傳最開始的位置，就絕對不能忽略它儀式性含意。或者說，左傳這方面像三易中的歸藏，從坤開始而不從乾開頭吧。即使這個故事有它歷史性的根據，我們還有足夠的理由認為，在地裡恢復母子關係的題目反映了當時的信仰以及儀式意識。

　　左傳中間部位的資料則更清楚了。從各方面，我們知道古代中國極爲重視在渾沌空間之中，建立一圈神聖，潔淨的秩序範圍。各種證據顯示當時的儀式措施，如禳於四門，磔，大儺等等(5)，爲了驅逐所有邪物，而將之推出圈外。在古中國神話當中，基於此儀式的「去四凶」的主題是廣被引用與發揮。而在左傳中的記載則較完整，因此誰都熟悉它的故事。可是據我所知，沒有人注意過在左傳裡「去四凶」的故事出現在文公最後一年（即〈文公十八年〉）的最後一部份；而〈文公〉是左傳裡的十二位諸魯公中的第六公。因此，「去四凶」的故事位於左傳的正中間，就像「去四凶」的儀式一樣，這個「去四凶」的故事像是在維持左傳裡篇章的前後排列的範圍。

眾所周知，春秋經的結尾是子路「結纓而死」。而孔丘亦一路走完。「西狩獲麟」之後，在左傳裡另外繼續敘述了接近十二年的混亂歷史才結束。

談到孔子的死亡，我們現在即能夠回顧到上面提的問題，而採取一種同時容納微觀與宏觀的看法。在春秋時代之前，周朝已經開始瓦解。左傳所記載的是諸侯的封建制度的逐步瓦解。雖然如此，春秋的末葉還是周朝的大聖人孔子在世的時候。孔丘則認爲，左丘明先生的傳文記載是最能夠讓人瞭解他自己的。因此，左傳的組織方面就反映著這個事實；差不多它三分之一，就是相當於它的「所見世」還加一點，則有這種不很明顯可是很重要的因素：它陪托相映著孔丘的生命。

這個問題，在傳統的註解上，就牽涉到「伏筆」的說法。一般來講，「伏筆」指聖人對於辭彙的選擇；被選的辭有某種程度或某種角度的意思，能傳達聖人對被記載人的行動的褒貶。因為這種概念強調選擇性，所以不採用的辭與被寫下的辭一樣傳達了意義。對於「伏筆」，我打算採取比較廣汎的定義；我也想要主張它的選擇性的基礎，可是我認為左傳的「伏筆」問題遠超於聖人判斷對方行為的道德價值。像傳統的「伏筆」的說法，我的也是基於聖人與其他世界的互相配合。我建議我們能視左傳為一種很微妙，很婉轉的證實，聖人的存在，即在這個混亂的世界，也具有他歷史上的回音。

因為這個假設既創新又複雜，因之本文的目標不以證明為鵠的。本人只想提出一些疑問，如果沒有別的適當的答案，則可視為需要類似此類假設成立的指標。大體上說，我要採用的方式是針對左傳敘述的分布性安排。要有系統性的進行這種研究，才能有滿意的結果；而系統性研究必定為艱鉅兼規模龐大。本文只能提出它的可能性而初步的描寫它的道理。

如以前述所言之方法我們就會問道：為甚麼孔丘的母親懷他的那年，左傳記載提出了「夏書曰。念茲在茲。釋茲在茲。名言茲在茲。允出茲在茲。惟帝念功。將謂由己壹也。信由己壹而後功可念也。」（〈襄，二十一年〉）的辭句？（雖然這是關於完全另外的故事，可是按照目前這「伏筆」的假設，這辭句應該解釋為「帝」對於未來聖人的降臨的祈禱）。而為甚麼那年的前後有那麼多關於解剖，分屍的事情？（例如：楚國薳子馮「闕地下冰而床焉」的故事，以準備〈襄，二十二年〉的「輬觀起於四竟」；「鯀殛 而禹興」；「使侯出諸轅轅」，這種地名就用上了下年要出現的這個「轅」字；「譬於禽獸。 臣食其肉。而寢處其皮矣」；而〈襄，二十 二年〉，孔子誕生的那年，除了「轅觀起於四竟」之外，也有蘧子馮講的「夫子所謂生死而肉骨也」（杜註：「已死復生。白骨更肉也。」）可見，這兩 年的資料值得多探究。）又爲甚麼〈襄，二十五年〉那麼強調「男女辨姓」，「男女以班」的事情？（〈襄，二十八年〉也出現一次「男女辨姓」。）

又爲甚麼孔子的第十七年（即〈昭，七年〉）突然出現一段「吾聞將有達者。曰孔丘。聖人之後也。」，敘述孔子祖先的德澤會遺傳在他身上。可見這個意思是孔子即將成年。值得注意的是種種神話性故事都記載在這年，尤其是與鬼神有關的。最奇怪的是在這段之後，有一小段關於衛侯傳位的問題。衛侯有兩子；因爲兄有足疾，因此立弟爲侯。值得琢磨的是：這情形頗似孔子本人的成年經歷。因爲孔丘之兄亦有足疾，因而孔子繼承了父系大宗。可見這情形即如論語所言：「魯衛兄弟之國也」。

又過十年，左傳的記載突然提起孔丘的教育過程（〈昭，十七年〉）。這年的故事除了很豐富的天文學資料（關於日蝕）之外，還有一段傳文，關於郯子對五帝的說法。他的說明應該算是一種「後圖騰代主義」理論；就是說，以他的「不能紀遠，乃紀於近」的概念，來架構古代神話世界與當代世界的基礎以及裂縫。上古的「圖騰社會」，經過郯子半雙關語性的解釋（「五鳩鳩民者也。五雉…雉民者也」等等），就傳達了古代社

13

會的精神。「於是仲尼年二十七」（杜注），就去向他學到這個知識。

又爲甚麼〈昭，二十七年〉的安排，連註家也會提出：「此傳多用自字」(6)？這個「自」的字，爲甚麼在這兒出現的頻率特別高呢？而爲甚麼下一年（即孔丘的第三十八年）所敘述的四件事件都是牽涉到美女之危？

這些疑問所給我們的暗示，就是古代中國社會裡的「年紀階級」制度的存在。早期傳統的社會就以年紀來劃分階級與群體的身份。關於這個制度的遺風，孔子自己所講的「吾十有五而志於學；三十而立；四十而不惑；五十而知天命；六十而耳順；七十而從心所欲，不踰矩。」（論語第二篇第四章），是一個例子；不過，禮記，〈曲禮〉則有更清楚的證據：「人生十年曰幼學。二十曰弱冠。三十曰壯有室。四十曰強而仕。五十曰艾服官政。六十曰耆指使。七十曰老而傳。八十九十曰耄…百年曰期頤。」。古代中國的男人，每十年左右就改變了一次地位。在二十與五十歲，甚至於名稱也改了；而從六十歲，所用來指他們，有「老」的意思的形容詞也是每十年都換一次。並且，重要的事蹟也安排在特定的年紀；就像周禮，〈媒氏〉曰「令男三十而娶，女二十而嫁」。在這樣社會制度之下，同年紀的小群都被分配在類似同樣的地位。因此，全社會的輪廓就擬似各人一生的經歷。這就是說，想要描寫社會的整體，或敘述各人生命中的事－陞A都能夠運用共同的架構；只不過，前者是以橫斷的角度看，而後者是以時流的次序爲主。

14

結構與事變

到現在，這篇文章走的方向，是由數目和時間的符號，這類形式上的象徵，而進到歷史上以及個人生活中的事蹟。可見，連個人經驗中的事變也會牽涉到結構性因素的考慮。既然我們的探討轉到這方面的問題，我們就不應該錯過最好的有關這個題目的參考資料。就是說，現在我們要討論一些關於易經的結構組織的問題。這當然又是一項需要很大規模的研究工作；因為這篇文章的目標是比較廣泛的，而它已經提出了足夠的尚未解決的題目；並且，因為易經的組織這個主題我已經在別的文章提供過某些線索與資料(7)，因此，在以下部份我打算只選擇比較基本的證據，來針對以上所疑問的難題從而採取新的角度而解釋。

所謂的結構組織，對易經而言，就是講到文王六十四重卦次序方面的問題。到現在為止，我們還沒有辦法說明，這六十四個卦在周易裡為甚麼作那樣的安排。雖然如此，就因為易經整體上的安排是明確的，我們便不能放棄對於這個問題的興趣。易經的次序絕對不可能是隨機湊集的。一眼看它的卦的形式上組織，就一目了然，設計這個構造是一件很艱難的創舉。話說回來，這個形式性秩序並不是能夠以數學的公式來描寫的，而是一種比較具體的，比較多元性的邏輯。設計周易的人採用的邏輯，比較起來應該是就著當時的宇宙觀而建立的。

現在我們就提一些最明顯的證據，來證明易經六十四文王卦是有整體上的次序安排。（一）易經最開始的兩個卦，並不是隨便任何甚麼卦都行，而是互相距離最大的。乾坤卦是互相區別最多的卦。而相反的，**易經**最後兩個卦，即既濟未濟卦，是全經裡陰陽爻相差最密集的卦（就是說，陽陰陽陰陽陰，陰陽陰陽陰陽）。這樣的排列難道不是經人精心安排過的呢？進一步講，它所描繪的形狀，應該是三角形的（它的基礎是相離最遠的兩卦，而它的頂頭則是相離最近的一對卦）。可見，當時的宇宙觀包含了這種三角形的空間。

（二）不但如此，這種三角形的架構也能夠分析的更仔細。分為上下經的**易經**具有以下的組織綱要：首先，有這基本的對立，乾對坤或天對地。跳過二十四個卦的話，到第二十七和二十八卦，就遇到一對具有對稱的卦，即頤和大過卦；當這種卦反轉的時侯，還是回到原來的型狀。因此，兩個卦不是互相以「相綜」的變法來演變的，而是互相以「相錯」來演變的。緊接者這對，就有一對關於水與火的卦。第二十九卦（坎卦）重復重疊「水」的三劃卦，而第三十卦（離卦）則重復用「火」的三劃卦。於是上經就結束了。

再說，下經是從「天地感而萬物化生」的咸和恆卦開始（代表開頭的乾坤卦的交往）。跳過二十八個卦的話，到第六十一和六十二卦，就遇到一對具有對稱的卦，即中孚和小過卦。這又是一對相錯的卦。緊接者，又是一對關於水與火的卦，就是「水火相濟」的既濟未濟卦。可見，在**易經**整體上，水與火不但是中間的轉扭，在最邊緣也是有一種超自然的混合情況。而中孚和小過卦則是進入那境界，開關著的「門」，一個通天的門，就像古時的「閶闔」一樣。

16

（三）我們來探究一下這種超自然的水火混合狀態。既濟未濟卦具有一種變形作用。如果把這兩個卦的十二個爻，一個一個把陰爻變爲陽爻，或陽爻變爲陰爻，結果，所出現的變卦，只有屬於以下三組的：（甲）第四十九和五十；（乙）第三，四，五，和六；以及（丙）第三十五，三十六，三十七，三十八，三十九和四十。（隨機選擇另外任何一對卦而加以這種變化操作的話，就不會產生如此整齊的結果。）這個變形作用的樞紐是青銅器時代最神聖的儀器（鼎卦），而另外它中部就通到一段在最開頭的卦（屯，蒙，需，訟卦），以及它外環通到一段在中間的卦（晉，明夷，家人，睽，蹇，解卦）。因此，從易經最頂頭所發出來的這種旋渦動態的變形作用，也算是在整體上構成一種折射形狀，而透到周易的基礎以及中間部位。

按：到現在，我們已經看過足夠的證據，讓我們能視水跟火爲敘述工具，適合於設置一個排列中間的轉振點。因此，我們可以回顧到前面遇到的問題。在左傳裡，孔丘的第三十年的資料特別强調「水火相濟」的主題。聖人孔子的一生是具有代表性的；可是問題是：是代表甚麼呢？假如古代社會本身早就含有一種典型的模型，以象徵各人應過的生活經歷，那麼後來的孔丘豈不沿者同樣的規格來設定自己的呈現呢？易經中的第三十位左右是屬於水火的，所以左傳在孔子三十年也設想水火的象徵了。我們在稍後就會比較仔細一點討論這方面的旁證。

（四）除了以上所考慮的例子，易經裡還有許多形式性的證據，能夠顯示出它的結構上的組織。在這裡，因爲限於篇幅，只再舉一次例。周

17

易的形式安排，從各種對稱現象都看得出來。比方說，從第七卦（師卦）到第十六卦（豫卦），這段含有十個卦的構造就彰顯出了一種很完美的對稱：設若中間的泰和否卦當中樞的話，其左右其他的卦就算是互相相反的（師和比卦，與同人和大有卦相錯，相當於小畜和履卦，與謙和豫卦相錯）。這種嚴格對稱關係絕不可能是隨機的；一定是經人故意安排的。

同樣的顯出被安排的次序，從第三十一卦到第四十卦一段（咸卦到解卦），在結構上頗像從第四十一卦到第五十卦那段（損卦到鼎卦）。尤其從第四十三卦開始，一直到第五十卦是一段完整的安排。先說這八個卦的「有對稱三劃卦」吧：從第四十三卦到第五十卦整整齊齊的列出來了「乾乾，坤坤，坎坎，離離」的三劃卦。而同時，這八個卦所呈現的不對稱的三劃卦，就是一再迭用「兌巽，兌巽，兌巽，兌巽」。要是加上這兩段各以互相相錯的卦而開始（即第三十一二卦，咸和恆卦，以及第四十一二卦，損和益卦），並且顧及前段的對稱與不對稱的三劃卦的分布，相當像後段的，我們就能夠很有把握的宣布這兩段的平行組織的答案。

這樣看，易經的形式上安排應該是不容懷疑的。可是它的結構不但是形式上（卦跟爻的佈置），也在它文詞上的象徵內容裡，經過過仔細的安排。它的形式與內容是同一體的。我們應該說，**周易是一種「宇宙藍圖」**。它不但是用文章討論一些哲學性的原理，而且在結構上明顯的體現當**時宇宙的組織。因此易經的各種形狀（特別是它的三角形形狀）包含當時宇宙的輪廓與特徵。從它文字上的象徵網的分布，可以歸納一年當中的四季循環（按：當然漢朝所盛行的算法－－卦氣，六日七分等等－－也有此說；目前所指的分布檢查有不同的基礎和結果。）；也可以歸納一個儀式的前後三個階段（就像禮記，〈郊特牲〉所言：「既灌然後迎牲」，易經在第二十卦（觀卦）有「盥而不薦」的辭句，然後在第二十九和三十卦就有關於犧牲的內容（「坎」是殺牲前為了接血所挖的溝；離卦裡就有全易經中唯一的一次用「折首」辭句），而到了第五十卦（鼎卦）才「鼎有實」）。再說，周易本身同樣的為古代社會各方面的基礎以及功能的模型。如果古代中國以年紀來劃分階級與群體的話，易經則應該保留遺跡。

我們拿這種以年紀劃分身份和群體的事，作假設來看易經吧。從開頭開始看做為父母的乾坤卦，接著是屯，蒙，需卦，都似乎可以配合這個假設（視為出生過程的描寫）。可是一遇到第六卦（訟卦）或者會有人說，難道六歲就吃官司嗎？其實不能這樣辯駁這種基於分配資料的假設。易經的邏輯是萬能，多元性的。除了象徵出生過程之外，這同一段也有關王的特權領域（聆聽訴訟，求雨，占卜，田獵，建諸侯，傳位（「克家」），聯婚，等等）。這些都與出生過程分配在第一到第十卦之內。要瞭解易經內任何一方的象徵，不能只從表面上一個一個例子看，而必須從整體上的分布資料來探究。

在古代中國，男人從四十歲「強而仕」到五十歲退役，這十年當中是最直接執政的年紀。對於易經五十卦（鼎卦）以後的象徵，我們稍後略作介紹。先掃視四十到五十卦的象徵排列，可以發覺那段關於行政制度方面的主題分布頗為密集；如制定日曆（革卦），高級物品的貿易（損益卦），計算記帳（損益），灌溉（困和井卦；另外夫和后卦也應解釋為牽涉到農業灌溉，水溝等等的問題）。同樣，這段中間兩卦（第四十五，四十六卦，即萃和升卦）也應該能夠解釋爲跟高層政府功能有關（開會，升台，儀式等等）。這些解釋暫時等到下一次有機會來寫。

男人「三十而娶」，從三十到四十歲是男人「壯有室」，就是男人成家的階段。因此易經裡的家人卦，才位於第三十七。另外，這段牽涉到太陽月亮晝夜的循環，以及家內烹飪方面的象徵，暫時不多發揮。現在要強調的是易經家人卦的相反：睽卦。睽卦辭中各種骯髒與不吉利的象徵，讓我們連想到家中各種水火不容的衝突。這種對立不異於左傳孔子三十七與三十八年所設立的：自己家內有夫人，家外有美人之危。

二十歲的男人要經過冠禮而後才成人。這個事實應該從三方面去瞭解：第一，冠禮作爲社會區分的符號；第二，它的教育意義；第三，成年儀式的考驗性質。在古代傳統的社會，個人平生隆重的事情，像成年和結婚，當然得運用各種符號從而表現社會上新的地位。男人二十歲所經過的冠禮有如此的社會功能；經過之後，他們才可以服兵役以及（當他們三十歲）結婚。而類似此禮，對女人而講則是笄禮；經過之後（在十五歲）才可以結婚（在二十歲）。易經裡唯一的一次提到類似「笄」的事情，就是在第十六卦（豫卦），九四：「朋盍簪」；這個象徵被位於此處可以作爲易經具有依照個人年紀的安排的重要證據。而下一個卦（第十七卦，隨卦）也有一些辭句，牽涉到成年的主題：如「係小子，失丈夫」，「係丈夫，失小子」等。這種情形，要是解釋爲青年人面對成長的挑戰所感到的恐懼與徬徨，就不會錯的太遠。並且，青年的複雜心理狀態，有可能產生像

20

蠱卦（第十八卦）裡所敘述的，各種腐敗的事情。總而言之，**易經**裡在第十七卦左右，**跟左傳**裡，孔丘第十七年的時候的記載，有不少符合的共同點。這是值得玩味的。

成年當然與教育有關。從經文記載，我們知道男人所受的教育，應該在一種男人會所之類的地方而進行。這種建築物有各種名稱，如序，庠，**學，密，辟廱**等。 這種制度就像一般傳統社會的男人會所。**易經**裡第二十卦（觀卦）就是體象著一個臺，也應該列入為這類會所之一。準備經過冠禮的男人在如此隔開的會所裡受的教育，當然要靠老師的教導，而拜師的條件是需送學費；當時做為學費的禮品是絲織品及束脩（其實這些禮品也是結婚禮物；因此我們可看出古社會教育與婚姻的相互依靠共同的功能）。在**易經**裡，代表束脩的莫過於第二十一卦（噬嗑卦）。它卦辭裡面提及各樣的肉類，如皮，腊肉，乾肉等等。其他在整部**易經**裡都無此類辭。而第二十二卦（賁卦）裡是全**易經**唯一提到「束帛」。我們怎麼能夠不承認這種線索是顯示當時的社會構造？

從人類學一般知識而言，傳統社會中的成年儀式大部份會演出一種象徵性的過程，就是成年者接受他屬於童年世界的自我的死亡，而再生於成人的世界；因此在傳統社會，常常進行成年考驗的儀式之後，才把新的地位給與青年。**易經**裡也有這類的架構，可憑為演出一種考驗的綱要的劇本。從噬嗑卦開始演吧：卦辭中所提到的束脩，可以說有引接老師的降臨；同時也引接老虎的降臨。這隻老虎的功能是兩面的：一方面，經過牠的

21

大口，讓成年者死而復生，這是牠凶的一面。另方面，老虎會保護那種神聖，潔淨的場所，而能驅逐所有邪物；這是牠的善的一面。（在各文化裡－－包括現代中國宗教的虎神－－，神話中的老虎常有這種兩面的功能）。易經的證據如下：噬嗑卦的九四明明是含在老虎嘴巴中的食物（「象曰：頤中有物曰噬嗑」）；這爻一變就至二十七卦（頤卦）：「虎視眈眈，其欲逐逐」（六四）。這是老虎對成年者所構成的威脅。而牠在善方面是基於頤卦對蠱卦的特殊關係。這就是說：蠱，噬嗑，頤，三卦有構成一種三角形，蠱與噬嗑卦是在觀卦左右建立著一個象徵對立為基礎，可以說這是腐敗與晒乾的肉的對稱（其實，仔細探討的話，這對立頗像周禮裡〈蠵人〉與〈臘人〉的對立）；而在頂頭上的頤卦則跟這基礎的左右角都有特殊關係。我們剛剛看過頤卦與噬嗑卦的特殊關係；對於頤卦與蠱卦的關係證據如下：（一）傳統的記載顯示老虎與蠱的敵對；（二）易經裡這兩卦是具有十個卦的一段的兩端；（三）在易經上經裡，隨和蠱卦，以及頤和大過卦是唯一的以兩個不對稱三劃卦而構成的。因此，我們有足夠的理由說，設計易經的人創造了一整套架構為了顯示成年的社會功能的意義。因此當左傳列出孔丘的第十七年以及第二十七年，成年和受教育的內容，就讓我們瞭解春秋時還有人保留傳達這種習俗。而且，這正像老子裡第二十篇(8)是全道德經唯一的地方提出「春登臺」有「臺」之類的辭句一樣。

我們不得不開始懷疑，古代中國的經文暗示我們一種曾為普遍性的象徵體系。

因為易經提供的模型是如此濃縮密集完整，對於做這種研究的人，它是一部關鍵性的證據。藉著它形式上的組織，我們才能夠瞭解當時歷史與結構是怎麼依靠數目而連繫的。就因為數目的邏輯系統具有那麼細密的規格，所以對這種分類宇宙觀範疇的構想而言，數字能夠作為最佳的原料。一言以蔽之，這種想法一開始就把數目看為實在的物品。以數目形成的宇宙觀結構，能變成人類經驗中各方面現象的基礎，因而就把那些現象加以抽象化。雖然如此，這種思考方式從未轉往出世的方向；所謂抽象化的過程總是在宇宙觀的範圍內。結果，這類的文化，則以劃分宇宙裡各層現象本有的結構為目的。這一層一層一系列的現象就同樣的參與數目的邏輯系統。甚至於，連計算數字也受了這種文化的影響；數目的排列所佔的概念空間也提供著可分類宇宙的機會與原料。時間也一樣在數目的網絡內被包容於空間化的特徵。而在這種空間和時間的座標之內，人生各方面的組織才能夠開始發生效果。政治以及其他社會構造也能夠靠這種結構體系而衍發功能。在這種媒體中，人類的經驗含有意義，而個人所經過的事變以及社會所經過的改變，就具有結構性道理可通。這些特點即是中國古代對結構與歷史的面目。

周易使我們能夠通到這些數目系統的組織。在這篇文章結束之前，我想舉最後一個例子，來證明古代經文的宇宙體系擁有多大的範圍。從前面所講的，我們知道，數目像實在的物品一樣；各個都有它獨有的品質與特徵。這樣想，第四十是個很有用的數目：因為四十（4 X 10）就算是四個整體，所以對於體現空間的四方等之類的現象就有用處。因此，易經的第三十九和第四十（蹇和解卦）這對卦，是整本周易裡，除了象徵大地的坤卦之外，唯一的地方提出「西南…東北」四方的名字 。（這樣看，蹇卦的「蹇」應視爲〈九歌，東皇太一〉裡的「靈偃蹇兮姣服」的蹇；而蹇卦辭的「往蹇來…」的公式即爲巫師向四方驅凶招福的儀式。因而，第四十卦的「解」字，除了註家的「鬆懈」的意思之外，也不得不滲入在四門所進行的「解開，解剖」之類的意境。）既然四十是個好數目，則五十就是更有用的；五十（5 X 10）畢竟比四十更加上中間的一點了。我們已經知道，在易經裡的第五十卦就是鼎卦；把最神聖的，最代表古代傳統文化的青 銅器，擺在第五十的位置是很明顯的帶著重要的意義。並且，鼎卦之後的下一個卦也提起「七鬯」之類很明顯的跟鼎的儀式背景符合的工具（下個艮卦的「艮」，我們不大清楚是甚麼玩意兒；可是假如像某些人講的，「艮」即「覲」，或像古歸藏寫的，是「狼」的意思，那麼就可以說第五十二卦就等著吃到鼎裡所薦的犧牲品吧）。易經裡從第五十卦到第六十卦所安排的其他的內容，暫時不必一個一個討論；大體上說，因爲有幾次提起「史，巫」等王朝中的官位（其實「豐」－－即那段中間的第五十五卦－－是西周的首都之一），所以我們如果設想這段爲社會最高層的地位與功能，就會有許多證據來支持此看法。

　　周易既然提供給我們這種線索，那麼我們何不乘這個機會來探討其他例子對於五十有甚麼樣子的表現？我們來找左傳與論語的證據吧。左傳

24

裡，敘述到孔丘的第五十年，就是〈定，八年〉；這年的記載包括「盜竊寶玉大弓」的故事。發生這個事件的場合是「禘於僖公」。在左傳裡，這個故事是有一點啼笑皆非的味道：事情亂到這個地步實在顯得無藥可救（而明年，陽虎還寶玉大弓的時候，當傳文解釋「得」與「獲」的區別，就暗示「獲麟」的「獲」，即孔子死亡的預兆）。這段記載既滑稽又悲哀。而它的中心象徵就是上古極神聖的「禘」祭。

易經的第五十位是最神聖的青銅器的鼎，而左傳裡，敘述孔丘的第五十年是寫上古的，拜高祖的禘典禮。而論語呢？如果我們一章一章的數論語的話，數到第五十條（即第三篇第十章），突然出現兩章關於禘的文章。這是整個論語唯一的地方提到「禘」字。怎麼那麼巧，這些紀錄都以「五十」的所在來佈置這種最高層的儀式象徵？

左傳與論語之所以有這種安排，是為了表示，雖然歷史的變遷已經促進了周朝很明顯的虧蝕，可是基本上這個文化還存在著；甚至於，用以記載這些虧蝕的象徵體系，本來就屬於那早期的文化。雖然經過了孔子的記載，表面上看，是在諷刺當時社會的退步，可是這些資料的組織含有正面的用意。關於孔丘的左傳以及論語，都保留著很多跟周易的連繫。

孟子曾經寫過：「孔子，聖之時者也」（〈萬章〉下一）。孔丘的舉動懂的配合時間性的條件；他會等到恰當的時刻才採取妥當的行動。我們也可以說，孔丘的一生，以及他遺留下來的經文，也是一種時間性的體象。對孔子而言，他的時代包含對他本人的存在有一種象徵性的回音。做為聖人的孔子，即能體現出他當時做人的典型。像這篇文章所提出的，古

25

代中國已經具有的宇宙觀，以及那個宇宙藍圖易經，而有充足的條件能~
成爲孔子時代的思想模型。

註

(1) 見 Bertrand Russell, "On the notion of cause, with application to the free-will problem", *Readings in the Philosophy of Science*, H. Feigl and M. Brodbeck, eds., (New York: Appleton-Century-Crofts, 1953), 387-407 頁.

(2) 就像尙書〈益稷〉的「予創若時，娶于塗山，辛壬癸甲 ，啓呱呱而泣」用這些符號來表示生產期的時間，我們很難不覺得天干最後的壬癸跟子有一種意義連繫，可以從壬之於妊，癸之於「癸水」的涵意去想。既然壬癸 能夠象徵生產，那麼所生的豈不是子呢？假如子本來就「屬於」壬癸（也許在甚麼「先天」的假設之下），那麼那種狀況就是一種天干地支各有平等的十一個單位；而「生子」之後才分成我們「後天」所熟悉的天干地支了。

(3) 見 島邦男，殷墟卜辭研究，（台北：鼎文書局印行，1975）, 293-294 頁.

註

(4) 見 Jay G. Williams, "On reading a Confucian Classic: The rhetoric of the *Lun Yu*", *Journal of Chinese Religions* (Fall, 1991), 19:105-111: "I, myself, am not at all convinced, however, that the *Lun Yu* is compiled randomly. On the contrary, my belief is that beyond the apparent chaos is a carefully contrived work with a unique rhetorical format designed to draw the reader into the Confucian *tao*. To be sure, the rhetoric of the *Lun Yu* is not that of Aristotle or of Xun Zi either. It is not a diachronic discourse designed to lead the reader through argument to one, author-contrived, conclusion. It is rather a matrix through which the reader, using his or her own creative skills learns to rebuild once more the Confucian edifice of wisdom." (106 頁).

(5) 見 栗原圭介 Kuriwara Keisike，磔禳 の 習俗 について Takujū no shūzoku ni tsuite，東方學 Tōhōgaku 45:12-28.

27

註

(6) 竹添光鴻，<u>左傳會箋</u>，下，第二十六卷，八頁。

(7) 見 「從結構觀點看易經的大小卦」，<u>鵝湖月刊</u> (1978), 9(6): 33-35 以及「古代妙器易經結構新窺」，<u>乾元</u>，（中國文化大學易學研究社） (1987), 2: 29-36.

(8) 這個算法當然是把〈道經〉擺在〈德經〉的前面。筆者當然知道這些篇段上的數字是很晚才出現的。

Structure and History: Remarks on Problems in the Composition of Ancient Chinese Classical Texts

Table of Contents

Irrespective of the properties of the external physical world, there must be human beings for there to be a cosmos. "Cosmos," our heaven-and-earth, thus comprises the world of physical objects enclosed within the human horizon, the inner world of the mind, and the cultural axes in our mutual world. The space of external objects does have its own time dimension; however, there must be a cosmos for there to be history. The characteristics which determine history are based upon its narrative properties. The conditions which constitute narrative must obtain for significance-holding events to be produced.

So, how do narrative properties such as meaning, plot, role, theme, focus, etc. come about? In the history of western philosophy, this question has received all kinds of replies; basically, in those such as reader reception theory, the emphasis is upon the way narrative effects arise from the reader's responses to the formal organization of the literature. This type of theory tends towards philosophical idealism, and runs the risk of over-emphasizing the subjective factors in reading. On the other hand, those theories which try to explain narrative effects as objectively existing qualities must face the difficulty of accounting for this external, independently existing state. Therefore, the most reasonable direction to take should be to adopt a theory of mutual interaction. Narrative properties depend upon human action and recognition in order to produce really objective qualities. In other words, these properties are contained and developed in the human cultural medium.

As Kant demonstrated, time and space are necessary, empty frames of human experience. For this reason, time must have the potential to be spatialized. The determination of the narrative properties of history is based upon the tri-segmentation of time into beginning, middle, and concluding periods. The meanings manifested by history are based upon the values of the beginning and middle sections being capable of being founded, for their own determination, on the values of the conclusion. We often discover that the beginnings of events narrated in history cannot be understood without knowing what their outcomes are. In the middle of things, the conclusion can modify the significance of their beginning. Thus, the middle region might become the pivot of the previous and the subsequent segments. This tri-segmental structure is very different from the causal relations of physical objects. It was just because the concept of causality was threatened with an infinite regress due to the lack of any ultimate mediating element, that Russell finally proposed the notion that causal relations are whatever regularities can be framed in any kind of functional expression[1]. It is only in a human-maintained cosmos that there are these sorts of tri-segmental narrative properties. Moreover, the sense of time is different from that of causality, in that it does not exclusively flow in a unidirectional way from before to after, from earlier to later. Rather, the significance of the present and of the past also possibly depends, for its determination, on the future.

The ancient classical literature of China is no exception to these formulations. If we aim at its organization through its narrative features, we will discover that the design of these ancient Chinese classics is based upon these sorts of properties. Due to the long monopoly of philology in the field of "Han studies," this sort of problem has been relatively neglected. In this essay, what I want to investigate is the analysis of the structural arrangement of ancient classical texts. I will provide some examples for discussion; although there will be more questions raised than answers supplied, perhaps this exercise can stimulate a recovery of academic interest in the holistic organizational structure of ancient classical texts.

---

[1] Russell, B. "On the notion of cause, with application to the free-will problem, "*Readings in the Philosophy of Science*, H. Feigl and M. Brodbeck, eds., (New York: Appleton-Century-Crofts, 1953), pages 387-407.

NUMBER SCIENCE

First, let's consider numbers. Logically speaking, numbers are simply sets whose elements can maintain progressive iterative relations, and which are capable of stepwise inclusion over the range of the sets. With appropriate work of definitional demarcation, these sets can organize quantitative relations between external, physical referents. At the same time, with the internal relations which are comprised by the various sets, there are various possibilities for operational procedures arising, which can be further developed within the rules of the system. However, ancient Chinese mathematics had some other kinds of goals in view. In ancient China, the most important application of number was to manifest the totality of the cosmos. For this reason, this type of tradition is very different from the typical early developments of applied mathematics, such as addition and subtraction, account-keeping, measurement, etc. The tradition of ancient Chinese mathematics rather emphasized the division of the symbolized whole cosmos into various types of sub-units. In this kind of operational system, there was a tendency not to clearly differentiate cardinal and ordinal numbers. The most important problem was not the magnitude of quantities, but rather was how to distinguish various kinds of sub-units, and which position to locate them in respect to the whole. Somewhat reminiscent of contemporary topology, ancient Chinese mathematical reasoning was not founded on questions of quantity, but rather on the overall distribution of forms over the surfaces of the totality.

Take, as an example, the first ten integers 1... to 10. Nine often is the symbol of universal domain in the cosmos; for instance, "Nine Places" represented all the world. However, nine is also ten: because this "nine," taken as a unitary whole, is also "one," and so nine in addition to its basic unitary totality equals ten. This sort of equation is often encountered in traditional Chinese thinking. At the same time, the series from one to ten must reflect various types of cosmological functions. The central 5, written in the ancient numerical script as an X, clearly displays its pivotal function. Five and six are just the central hinge for a rotation joining the previous and the subsequent numbers; when this pivot takes place, the sum of these numbers is eleven, and all the numbers joined in the space defined by this operation also sum to eleven (4 + 7, 3 + 8, 2 + 9...). This is a basic teaching of the *Hetu* and *Loshu*, as everybody knows. So, traditional Chinese mathematics were inseparable from this sort of magic square conceptualization.

CALENDRICAL TEMPORALITY

Next, consider the "Heavenly Stems and Earthly Branches." To coordinate ten symbols with twelve other symbols in order to record temporal duration is already to inscribe structure on the flow of time. What should command even more attention is that these symbols were not simply abstract markers, but rather had already long been carriers of symbolic meaning. Under the premises of the ancient cosmology, this schematism reveals some of the contours and anatomy of the view of the cosmos at the time. To speak of the "Heavenly Stems," the connotation of *jia* makes it difficult not to associate with cosmological functions such as opening out, issuing forth, giving birth, etc. And *yi*, then, means returning, coming back; this is analogous to the contrastive meaning of the hexagrams Qian and Kun at the beginning of the *YiJing*. As for the "Earthly Branches," the placement of *zi* at the beginning of this series is a very suggestive bit of data[2]. And in the center of these series, located at the position corresponding to "Snake" in the "Twelve Animal Cycle," *ji* and *si* are both at locus number six. Just the

[2] Just as is stated in the YiJi chapter of the *ShangShu*, "I... married TuShan, *xing, ren, gui, jia*, Qi noisily squalled": this uses these markers to express the time of gestation. We have difficulty not thinking that *ren* and *gui*, the last symbols of the Heavenly Stems, along with *zi*, have this sort of meaningful connection; which can be seen as implied in the relation of *ren* with "pregnant," *gui* with "menstrual flow," etc. Since *ren* and *gui* can symbolize birth, it stands to reason that what is born is the "child" (*zi*). If *zi* originally "belonged" to *ren* and *gui* (perhaps in some sort of hypothesis of a time "Before Heaven"), then that sort of condition would imply that the Heavenly Stems and Earthly Branches each had eleven units then; and only after "giving birth to the child (*zi*)" would there be some sort of "After Heaven" arrangement of the Heavenly Stems and Earthly Branches with which we are familiar.

shape of these characters themselves already displays the features of pivotal rotation and superimposition of the previous and the subsequent markers (do the forms of *ji* and *si* not seem serpentine?).

What is more, we cannot refrain from asking about the forgotten meanings of *ding* and *mao* in the fourth position of the "Heavenly Stems and Earthly Branches." *Ding* was written as a dot, whereas *mao* was written as the dot, split into two halves. *Mao* referred to a type of sacrificial ceremony where animals were killed—probably cut in some way—and offered[3]. And in a cosmology such as that of the Shang Dynasty, where the number "four" was of great importance (four directions, four seasons, etc.), the fourth position should not be without its special characteristics (questions such as: in the center of the four directions, does the point in the middle count as an independent position, or not? and so forth). *Ding* and *mao*, coordinated together here, must have this type of implication: "unitary yet dual, dual yet unitary," inasmuch as *ding* is a whole, a point, and *mao* is this point divided into two split parts. These symbols must have been associated in some way, in some common background. In sum, besides being a mathematical tool, the "Heavenly Stems and Earthly Branches" also had

---

[3] See, Shima Kunio, *YinXu BuCi YanJiu*, (Taipei: DingWen Publishing, 1975), pages 293-94.

mythological character. And in the relations which ramified in the symbolic networks they constituted, they were still able to develop the ways of their narrative cosmology.

AN IDEALIZED STATE

Do governmental functions have this sort of order? Everybody knows that the *ZhouLi* is a book which has undergone thorough and extensive adjustment, but few have examined its structural arrangement. What is interesting is that in the *ZhouLi*, even the most trivial services can display the axes or categories of ancient Chinese cosmological classification. For instance, what's the King of the *ZhouLi* going to eat? The chapter "Offices of Heaven" describes a whole roster of personnel dedicated to providing the king with the means of gustatory satiety. Altogether, there are ten positions, as follows: the Chefs, the Kitchen Workers, the Inner and Outer Feast Attendants, the Maitre d', the Field Master, the Game Man, the Fisherman, the Man of Aquatic Creatures, the Pemmican Man. From any number of perspectives, this list shows a rigorous formal structure. It is quite obvious that these ten positions divide into a first and second half. The first two pairs are closer to the "inside"; the Chefs and Kitchen Workers (both given titles ending in *fu* in the original text) are by degrees arrayed near the fire, doing the culinary work. Next to them,

37

there are two roles which attend to the "feast," which are also arrayed from inner towards outer. The last four positions in the list are all called Such-and-such "Man," and they are responsible for providing various kinds of game for food; thus, compared with the first half, they are relatively "outside," relatively "peripheral" or "natural." In these four units, there is also a very careful organization evident. Actually, they are also listed by pairs: their domain and importance becomes smaller and slighter as they proceed. The game hunted on land is to the fish caught in the water, as the small "creatures of mutuality" (clams, turtles, etc.) from the water are to the dried or roast pemmican. The job description of the Pemmican Man at the end of these four units includes mention of the contribution the Game Man is responsible for; in fact, preparing pemmican depends on game meat. The Game Man's job description is to provide wolf in winter, to provide a kind of deer in summer, and in "spring and autumn" to provide "game." That is, summer and winter are clearly distinguished seasons, and the seasons of spring and autumn are unmarked (not distinctly separated), so the animals designated for these seasons are also generalized and undifferentiated. Whereas, the Fisherman's work is assigned to springtime, and the Man of Aquatic Creatures provides tortoises and clams in spring, as well as turtles and fish in autumn. The Pemmican Man relies upon the Game Man, and is thus not given an assigned temporal locus. It is very evident that whoever arranged this list took pains at the time in considering the details of its construction.

The two positions in the center are rather special. The Field Master is the only one in the entire series to be called the "Master" of anything, and as well, his is the only role which involves the provision of agricultural products. The Maitre d' evinces a kind of pivotal function: although he is placed in the first half of the list, his title bears the character of Such-and-such "Man" which we saw is characteristic of the positions in the last half of the list. Moreover, the Maitre d' and the Field Master have a special responsibility towards fire and water. Particularly, the Maitre d' is explicitly assigned a relation towards "water and fire." That this roster has ten units, and that at its center the characters "water and fire" are displayed, is not at all an accidental occurrence. At the time, the personnel who served the Son of Heaven in his daily life, were absolutely not casually set up; they carried the symbolism representing the whole cosmos in their arrangement. In this way, each of them, in their own proper rankings, participated in the cosmos of their time.

THE THOUGHTS OF A SAGE

To this point, the topics that we have been discussing can be fairly easily imagined to involve connections with structural factors. Symbols concerning number, time, or government of course have to do with formal considerations. Now, however, we are going to investigate a different kind of phenomenon. Will such a work as the *Lun Yu*, that record of pronouncements of the Sage, similarly comprise structural organization? What this question aims at is the holistic, overall design of ancient classical texts. Before we analyze a few examples, we should first think of what name we should give to this domain of scholarly enterprise. According to Aristotle's division of basic scholarship, there were three areas, called Grammar, Logic, and a third (called Rhetoric) which taught students how to argue properly; while this latter discipline is now translated in Chinese as "the study of embellished words," it might more appropriately be translated as "persuasive technique." Contemporary literary studies no longer restrict this specialization to treating only questions of convincing a debating opponent, but rather under the rubric of rhetoric deal with a wide variety of issues concerned with narrative strategies. As far as our present problem is concerned, we can say: superficially, the *Lun Yu* appears to consist simply of one entry listed after another. However, as also has been suggested by others, perhaps the sequence of sentences or paragraphs expresses some sort of ordered connection[4]. The circumstance certainly allows for some hypotheses and speculations. In the present essay it will not be possible to treat carefully the question of the arrangement of the *Lun Yu*; we will simply be able to bring forward a few clues and hints.

In fact, the arrangement of entries in the body of the *Lun Yu* does not really seem to be totally random. For example, *Lun Yu* 14.27 and 14.28 are obviously related by common ideas and vocabulary: "Those not in the position should not plan the strategy" and "The lordly person's thinking does not exceed his position." Because the first of these is a repetition of 8.14, so this type of arrangement probably was due to an association made at the time of the book's editorial compilation.

Once again, at *Lun Yu* 8.3 through to 8.7, these five entries are all concerned with "Zengzi was ill" and then his death. If the classic were compiled randomly, then why would these passages, which are all related, be linked together like

---

[4] See, Jay G. Williams, "On reading a Confucian Classic: The rhetoric of the *Lun Yu*," *Journal of Chinese Religions* (Fall, 1991), 19:105-111: "I, myself, am not at all convinced, however, that the *Lun Yu* is compiled randomly. On the contrary, my belief is that beyond the apparent chaos is a carefully contrived work with a unique rhetorical format designed to draw the reader into the Confucian *tao*. To be sure, the rhetoric of the *Lun Yu* is not that of Aristotle or of Xun Zi either. It is not a diachronic discourse designed to lead the reader through argument to one, author-contrived, conclusion. It is rather a matrix through which the reader, using his or her own creative skills learns to rebuild once more the Confucian edifice of wisdom." (page 106)

this? This sort of phenomenon probably was not the result of any subsequent editing during the time of compilation, and reflects the fact that these several sentences were originally all joined together in the first place.

There are lots of examples of such circumstances in the *Lun Yu*. For instance, 13.8 and 13.9, although the points are slightly different in their intended significance, nonetheless both are concerned with problems of "wealth" (*fu*), and both array the point dealing with "wealth" in the third segment of the respective argumentative series. It can be readily seen in this way that the question of narrative effects in the *Lun Yu* is not without some basis in factual evidence. In this way, we realize that any attempt to investigate this type of hypothesis will of necessity have to adopt some kind of method based upon the phenomena of distribution in the text.

Furthermore, *Lun Yu* has yet another kind of narrative property. The persona who appear in its pages often will perform a similar style of role whenever they appear. Yan Hui, Zi Lu, and other disciples, each has his own set role. Fan Chi is another very clear example. The topics which appear in conjunction with this man include: sacrificial offerings, death, burial, ghosts and spirits, the "dancing cloud" rain altar, agriculture, birth and growth, etc.—all of a rather concrete organic and religious flavor. For this reason, when Fan Chi asks about "humanness and knowledge" (6.20) and is answered in terms of ghosts and spirits, then the following passage, which talks of "the person of knowledge takes pleasure in water, the person of humanness takes pleasure in mountains," should really be taken as linked together with the previous one, so that they are read continuously without a break. Looking at the entire set of evidence this way, Fan Chi, as a person, carries somewhat of the general ambience of the ancient nature religion.

HISTORICAL STRUCTURE

Indications such as these are plentiful. Presently we are in no position properly to achieve any conclusion; our goal can merely be to point to the existence of the problem. The records of the utterances of the sage are also susceptible of being collected and assembled according to a formal arrangement. However, history to the contrary is not necessarily the same way. The events that happen in the flow of time should be the epitome of random occurrences, and so the history that records them also, by all rights, ought not to have any inherent structure. Inspite of this, if we look at the *Chronicles of Zuo*, we will begin to have our doubts about this proposition.

Having said this, it must immediately be stated clearly that the topic presently at hand is not one of the verity or accuracy of the historical documents recorded in the *Chronicles of Zuo*. The investigation of whether its historical material really corresponds with the events that happened at the time would have to proceed on an entirely different plane. We know that at the time in China, the aristocratic rulers of almost every little feudal state each employed a department of specialists to inscribe its history, to record its important events. Our present problem has nothing to do with the relation of this material to its external referents in the outside world; rather, what we want to investigate is the internal organization of the *Chronicles of Zuo* itself. It does not matter where these stories have come from; the question we must ask is: why is the historical material, which has been selected to appear under a certain year of chronicle, just this material and not some other? If we think about it, we will discover that in the *Chronicles of Zuo* there are many places which, if we take them as being straightforward historical accounts, are not very easily understood as such. It is just because it makes the claim of being history that the problem of its internal organization becomes so apparent.

The techniques used by the *Chronicles of Zuo* to narrate the Spring and Autumn period's history have already met wide acclaim. Particularly the passages narrating warfare are especially famous, to the extent that what most captures many readers' attention are the portions dealing with great wars of the Spring and Autumn period. Moreover, the *Chronicles of Zuo* convey with great clarity the daily frictions, evolution and internal structural conflict of the society of its time. Everyone who reads the *Chronicles of Zuo* will appreciate how this book acutely depicts the fact that the temperaments and attitudes of individuals play a very important role in the developments of history. Stories in the *Chronicles of Zuo* often employ extraordinarily subtle details to make manifest how the frame of mind of individuals, or the early dynamics of events in an incipient situation, can take on very great significance when considered in terms of their outcomes in the future. Also, events in the future can possibly influence the disposition of present events. For example, in the 6th year of Duke Wen, Duke Mu of Qin had human sacrifices performed at his funeral, and for this reason, "The lordly person says: 'It is fitting that Mu of Qin was not the leader of the alliance!'" This is to say that later events can be used to explain earlier situations. For this reason, the *Chronicles of Zuo* is everywhere charged with the significance of an atmosphere heavily fraught with fate. Whoever is willing to read the *Chronicles of Zuo* as a whole, and not simply in excerpted stories, will enjoy this wonderful narrative skill, which shows the complexly layered interconnections which make up history, and in their mutual influences and interweavings, will share the deep, thickly-deposited sense of temporal flow that has been left by ancient China.

These marvelous narrative effects are based upon some of the more usual historical characteristics. Besides temporality, motive, development, and so on—these narrative elements which are universal within human interaction—in the *Chronicles of Zuo* there is another type of structural problem involved, which can be seen in such occurrences as its common use of parallel organization. For instance, in the 11th year of Duke Wen, in the quite short chronicles of the same year, there are two occasions of a narrative element such as "bury his head at (such-and-such) gate." Of course, the second mention of this phrase is during an instance of the "retrospective narration" for which the *Chronicles of Zuo* are famous ("In the beginning, in the age of Duke Wu of Song..."); and it is employed in working up a preparation for events which will happen in the future in the 30th year of Duke Xiang; nonetheless, from the viewpoint of its narrative properties, there must be some definite motive behind selecting just this detail for arrangement in the locus of this year's material. However, the chronicle text for this year is rather corrupt and contains several obvious errors. If one felt compelled to make up some sort of hypothesis, no matter how forced and unconvincing, one might say: we know that in other places, reduplicated text is definitely erroneous; for example, in the *Spring and Autumn Classic* for the 21st and 24th years of Duke Xiang, each year writes two instances of "solar eclipse" in the records. We certainly know that in one year there are not so many solar eclipses visible, so self-evidently it is certain that there are some extraneous characters among these documents. Perhaps a reduplicated phrase such as "bury his head at (such-and-such) gate..." can also be accounted for as an accident which happened some time during the editing and compilation of the chronicle commentary.

If we consider the parallel organization of the *Chronicles of Zuo* one more time, we will have to abandon this kind of hypothesis. There are a good many examples which feature duplicated details. For one: in the 13th year of Duke Cheng, it is obvious that there are two stories featuring the following sequence: (1) Somebody has the responsibility of going to carry out some sort of ceremonial procedure; (2) he is "disrespectful"; (3) Somebody else lectures about ceremony ("Ceremony is the trunk of the body") or about respect ("To work hard at ceremony, there's nothing like full respect"); (4) And in conclusion uses a phrase such as, "Slack. Abandons the lord's [his] order." It is uncertain whether we should say that in the year 578 B.C. everybody spoke using the same sentence patterns (of course this is a possibility), or whether it was that Mr. Zuo QiuMing, in editing and compiling the materials for the 13th year of Duke Cheng, wanted to make this year reveal its connection with just these sorts of problems.

Because this kind of example is so numerous, we will not go through mentioning them one by one. Let's just use a last example to begin to raise the issue of why a certain type of parallel organization might "belong" to a certain year in the chronicle commentary. The 20th year of Duke Zhao was 522 B.C.; that is to say, it was the thirtieth year since Kong Qiu was born. The material from this year is very abundant; in it there is the talk Yanzi gives about "Whether harmony is different from sameness?". When Yanzi replies to this question he extrapolates to aspects of cooking, and so naturally he mentions "water and fire" as factors in his explanation. Actually, the mutual complementarity of fire and water is a rather important metaphor throughout this entire presentation, since its conclusion includes the phrase, "It's like using water to complement water: nobody would eat that." Immediately following this discussion there is a segment where the Marquis of Qi asks about "Ancient and undying." What is really strange is that the episode right after this is where Zi Chan dies, and the last words he utters before his death are also a disquisition upon the theme of fire and water. After that, Kongzi goes on developing the thoughts about harmony which were under consideration in the earlier section. Now, why would the 20th year of Duke Zhao give this much prominence to the symbols of fire and water?

This type of evidence should serve to heighten our awareness of the structural organization of ancient history. However, the range of this problem is not limited to the arrangement of material year by year. Other than this type of micro-scale arrangement, we should also not neglect the aspect of macro-level, holistic organization. Besides being a segment of history, it is also a cosmology which has an overall structure. It is beyond doubt that the *Chronicles of Zuo* have set up three special regions: i.e., their beginning, their middle, and their conclusion. Each region provides us with some cues, for us to pay attention to the *Chronicles of Zuo*'s background in the culture of ritual. It cannot be denied that the first year of Duke Min, from the very beginning story, obviously establishes this type of ritual context. Although the quarrel, separation, and reconciliation of Duke Zhuang of Zheng and his mother Jiang Shi, taken superficially, may not necessarily imply any deeper level of meaning, yet when one takes into consideration the major premise of the story, and its execution—that is, the oath, "we'll not meet again unless it's at the Yellow Springs"; the clever solution, "furrow the earth until the spring is reached"; and the stereotypical behavior and formulaic speech involved in passing through the trench and reciting onomatopoeic verse—and when one adds to this the consideration that this story is located at the very beginning of the *Chronicles of Zuo*, then it is absolutely clear that the ritualized implication of the story is not to be overlooked. Perhaps it could be said that in this respect the *Chronicles of Zuo* resemble the *Gui Cang* version of the three ancient Classics of Change (of which only the *YiJing* survives), in that they begin with Kun (the earth hexagram) and not Qian (the sky hexagram). Even if this story has its historical basis, we have sufficient reason to recognize that this theme of recovering the mother-son relation by returning within the earth must reflect the beliefs and ritual consciousness of its time.

The material of the middle of the *Chronicles of Zuo* is even more clear. We know in many ways that ancient Chinese took serious steps to establish, in the middle of chaotic space, a circular domain which was sacred, cleansed, and orderly. From many sources, we are shown the ritual measures which were used at the time, such as the dismemberment offerings at the four gates, the various other rites featuring dismemberment for exorcistic purposes, the Great Nuo ceremonies, etc.[5]; the intent

---

[5] Kuriwara Keisike, "Takujû no shûzoku ni tsuite" *Tôhôgaku* 45:12-28.

of such rituals was to drive away all evil or pollution beyond the sacred territory established by the ceremonies. In ancient Chinese mythology, the theme of "Exorcising the Four Monsters," which is based on such ritual, is widely cited and developed. And in the *Chronicles of Zuo* text, the version of this myth is relatively fully realized, so everybody knows this story. However, as far as I know, nobody has ever paid attention to the fact that, in the *Chronicles of Zuo*, the story of "Exorcising the Four Monsters" appears in the last part of the last year of Duke Wen (i.e., the 18th year of Duke Wen). And "Duke Wen" is the sixth duke in the series of twelve dukes from the state of Lu in the *Chronicles of Zuo*. Therefore, the story of "Exorcising the Four Monsters" is located in the exact center of the *Chronicles of Zuo*. Just like the ritual "Exorcising the Four Monsters," this story of "Exorcising the Four Monsters" seems to be maintaining the domain of the textual order, in its arrangement of previous and subsequent passages.

As everybody knows, at the conclusion of the *Spring and Autumn Annals*, Zi Lu "ties the tassel and dies." And Kong Qiu also has come to the end of his road. After "a unicorn is obtained in the western hunt," the *Chronicles of Zuo* go on narrating nearly twelve more years of chaotic history, before coming to an end.

Speaking of the death of Kongzi, we now are able to return our attention to a problem raised earlier, using a point of view which combines both the micro-level and macro-level of analysis at the same time. Before the Spring and Autumn period, the Zhou Dynasty had already begun to disintegrate. The records of the *Chronicles of Zuo* present the gradual disintegration of the feudal lords' aristocracy. Although this is so, the waning age of the Spring and Autumn period were the years when the great Sage of the Zhou Dynasty, Kongzi, was in the world. And Kong Qiu held that the commentary which Mr. Zuo QiuMing had recorded were the best means of having others get to understand him. For this reason, the organizational aspects of the *Chronicles of Zuo* reflect this fact; almost one-third of it, that is the part corresponding to its "witnessed world" plus a bit more, has this not very obvious but very important factor: it accompanies and reflects the life of Kong Qiu.

In traditional commentaries, this problem comes to involve the thesis of "hidden messages." "Hidden messages" refers to the Sage's choice of vocabulary; the selected lexical item carries a certain degree or angle of significance, to convey the praise or blame of the Sage towards the actions of the people recorded. Because this kind of concept emphasizes selectivity, the vocabulary not selected just as much conveys significance as that which is written down does. I plan to adopt a broader definition of "hidden messages"; I also want to emphasize its basis in selectivity, but I believe that in the *Chronicles of Zuo*, "hidden messages" go far beyond the issue of the Sage's judgements of moral value concerning the behavior of other people. Just like the traditional notion of "hidden messages," mine also is based on the mutual coordination of the Sage and the rest of his world. I suggest that we can see the *Chronicles of Zuo* as a kind of very subtle, very indirect demonstration that, even in a world that has been thrown into chaos, the existence of the Sage has its historical echo.

Because this hypothesis is both new and complex, the goal of the present essay cannot be to prove it. I want only to raise a few questions; if there are no other satisfactory answers to these, then this should be taken as an indication that some sort of similar hypotheses need to be established. Basically, I want to employ an approach which aims at the distributional arrangement of the *Chronicles of Zuo* narratives. This research needs to be pursued systematically before satisfactory results can be achieved, and systematic research will be both arduous and expansive in scale. This essay can merely mention its possibility and make a preliminary attempt to describe its rationale.

According to the methods just discussed, we would be able to ask: Why, in the year in which Kong Qiu's mother was pregnant with this child, do the records in the *Chronicles of Zuo* cite the following: "The *Book of Xia* states: 'Think this by this; release this from this; name this by this; this confidence emerges from this. Only the Lord's intentional thought is efficacious. Imminent speech is emitted from the unified self; confident expectation is emitted from the unified self, and afterwards, the efficacy can be thought."? (21st year of Duke Xiang. Although this concerns a totally different set of circumstances, according to the present "hidden messages" hypothesis, these phrases would be interpreted as the "Lord's" incantatory prayer for the imminent descent of the future sage.) Also, in the years around this time, why are there so many references to dismemberments? (E.g., in the feudal state of Chu, Wei ZiPing "furrows the earth, lies and makes his bed on the ice," in preparation for next year's story (22nd year of Duke Xiang) concerning "using horses to pull apart GuanQi in four directions"; "Gun was dismembered and Yu arose"; "he had the Marquis go out to HuanYuan," which uses the same word for a place name as the word meaning "using horses to pull somebody part" to be used in the next year; "it's like hunting game; I eat its meat, and sleep in its pelt"; and in the 22nd year of Duke Xiang, the year that Kongzi is born, other than "using horses to pull apart GuanQi in four directions," there is also Wei ZiPing's words: "What my master says makes the dead come back alive and puts meat back on the bones" (the Du Yu commentary explains: "Something already dead returns to life. White bones are once again covered with meat."). Clearly, the material in these two years deserves much more intensive examination.) Furthermore, why does the 25th year of Duke Xiang so emphasize matters such as "separate lineage names of men and women" or "men and women were separated"? (In the 28th year of Duke Xiang there also appears one instance of "men and women have separate lineage names").

And again: why, in Kongzi's seventeenth year (i.e., the 7th year of Duke Zhao), does there suddenly appear a section about, "I have heard that there will be an achiever, named Kong Qiu, the descendent of a sage", which narrates Kongzi's ancestral reserve of virtue which will be inherited in his lifetime? Obviously, the meaning of this is that Kongzi is about to mature to adulthood. What is worth paying attention to is the many stories with mythological details recorded in this year, especially ones concerning ghosts and spirits. The most peculiar aspect of this year's chronicle is that after this section on Kong Qiu, there is a short segment concerning the transmission problems of the Marquis of Wei. The Marquis of Wei had two sons; because the older son had an infirmity in one leg, so it was decided to set up the younger son as heir. It is worth considering that this situation is really very similar to Kongzi's own experience in attaining adulthood. Because Kong Qiu's older brother had an infirmity in one leg, Kongzi was chosen to continue the patriline as heir. Clearly, this situation is like what the *Lun Yu* says: "The feudalities of Lu and Wei are brother states!"

Once again, ten years later, documents in the *Chronicles of Zuo* suddenly mention Kong Qiu's educational process (in the 17th year of Duke Zhao). Besides abundant material on astronomy (concerning solar eclipses), the stories in this year also include a stretch of commentary dealing with Tanzi discussing his notion of the Five Lords. His explication ought to be considered a type of "post-totemistic" theory; that is, using the concept of "not being able to record the distant, then record the proximal," he sets up the way the ancient mythological world grounds the present world, and yet the hiatus which has since been introduced between them. The "totemistic society" of antiquity, when seen in the light of the half-punning explanations Tanzi offers ("The five pigeons (*ji*) assembled (*ji*) the people; the five hawks (*zhi*)... regulated (*yi* (in the archaic language a cognate with *zhi*)) the people"), conveys

56

the archaic spirit of ancient society. "At this point, Zhong Ni was in his 27th year" (Du Yu's commentary), and he went to learn this knowledge from Tanzi.

Again, why is the 27th year of Duke Zhao arranged in such a fashion that even the commentators point out "There are many instances of the character for 'self' (*zi*) being used in this [year's] commentary"[6]? Why does this *zi* character appear with such a high frequency just in this place? And why in the next year (that is, the 38th year of Kong Qiu) do all four stories narrated here involve the dangers of beautiful women?

These questions suggest to us the presence of an age-grade system in ancient Chinese society. Early traditional societies based status and group distinctions on the age of the cohort. Some last vestiges of this custom were evidenced in Kongzi's own words, "When I was fifteen, I set my heart-and-mind towards learning; at thirty I took my stance; at forty I was no longer of two minds; at fifty I heard the orders of heaven; at sixty my ear was attuned; at seventy could follow what my heart-and-mind wanted and not overstep the guidelines" (*Lun Yu*, 2.4); but the evidence of the QuLi chapter of *LiJi* is even clearer: "From the beginning of human life, and after ten years,

6 Takezoe Kôkô , *ZuoZhuan HuiJian* (Taipei: Fenghuang Publishing, 1977 (1903)), volume 2, chapter 26, page 8.

this is called youthful and learning; twenty is weak capping; thirty is robust and having a household; forty is strong and serving in government; fifty is old and official service; sixty is very senior and commanding; seventy is elderly and delegating; eighty and ninety are extremely aged... one hundred is awaiting nourishment." Men in ancient China changed their status every ten years. At the twentieth and fiftieth years, they even changed their names; and from the age of sixty, the adjective used to describe them as "old" also was revised each ten years. As well, important life events were also arranged at specially designated ages, such as stated in the MeiShi chapter of *ZhouLi*, "Have the men marry at thirty, the women marry at twenty." In this sort of social system, the age groups were each assigned to similar positions. For this reason, the overall social outline approximated the experience of an individual's lifetime. That is, to describe the whole of society, or to narrate the events of an individual's lifetime, one is always able to use a common framework; only, the former is considered synchronically, while the latter emphasizes a diachronic order.

STRUCTURE AND EVENT

To the present point, the direction this essay has traversed has gone from the formal symbolism of markers of number and of time, and proceeded to historical events and the events of individuals' lifetimes. Clearly, even the happenstance of individual experience involves consideration of structural factors. Since our investigation has turned in the direction of these questions, we should not leave out the best resource material for this sort of issue. That is, now we will discuss some questions having to do with the structural organization of the *YiJing*. Of course, this is once again a project needing very large-scale research. Because the present essay has a rather broader purpose, and has already brought up enough topics which still await resolution—and also because the present author has already written some essays about the organization of the *YiJing*, in which some clues and material were offered[7] —so in what follows here, I plan simply to choose some rather basic evidence, and to aim it at the questions already raised, in order to resolve some of the difficulties, by using a new perspective for the explanation.

In relation to the *YiJing*, what is meant by "structural organization" has to do with questions about the order of the sixty-four hexagrams arranged in the "King Wen" sequence. Until the present time, there has not been any way to explain why the sequence of hexagrams in the *ZhouYi* which we have today has

---

[7] See "Cong Jiegou Guandian Kan *YiJing* de DaXiao Gua", *EHu YueKan*, (1978), 9(6):33-35; and "Gudai Miaoqi *YiJing* Jiegou Xinkui", *QianYuan* (Zhongguo Wenhua Daxue *YiJing* Yanjiushe) (1987), 2:29-36.

received the order of arrangement that it has. Although it has not been explained, we cannot abandon our interest in this question, just because the *YiJing* clearly has been given an overall arrangement. One look at the formal organization of the hexagrams makes it very evident that to execute the design of this apparatus was quite a monumental creation. On the other hand, this formal order really cannot be described by a mathematical formula; it is a more concrete, more pluralistic logic than that. The logic adopted by the designers of the *YiJing*, comparatively speaking was more akin to the cosmology in effect at the time.

Now we will adduce a few quite obvious pieces of evidence to prove that the order of the sixty-four King Wen hexagrams of the *YiJing* has an overall arrangement. (1) The first two hexagrams of the *YiJing* are not just any random pair, but rather are the two which are the most mutually distant. Qian and Kun hexagrams are maximally differentiated from each other. And, conversely, the last two hexagrams in the *YiJing* are Ji Ji and Wei Ji hexagrams, the most mutually integrated hexagrams in the entire classical text (that is, their lines most closely intertwine *yang* and *yin* lines). This sort of array must have been the result of somebody's deliberate arrangement. Moreover, the shape which it describes should be a triangular one (its base is formed by the points of the pair of hexagrams at the farthest distance one from the other, while its apex is formed by the pair of hexagrams closest one to the other). Obviously the cosmology of that time must have included this kind of triangular or pyramidal space.

(2) Not only that, but this kind of triangular frame can be analyzed in even more detail. The organization of the *YiJing*, which is divided into a first and second half, has the following outline: first, there is this basic oppositional pair, Qian versus Kun or heaven paired with earth. Jumping over twenty-four hexagrams, hexagrams #27 and #28 are symmetrical hexagrams: when they rotate or flip over, they still retain their original form. For this reasons, these two hexagrams are related to each other by inverting the lines, rather than (as most hexagrams are) by rotation. Immediately following this couple, there is a pair of hexagrams which concerns water and fire. Hexagram #29 (Kan, The Pit) is the water trigram doubled, while #30 (Li, The Clinging) is the fire trigram doubled. At this point, the first half of the classic comes to an end.

Then, the classic's second half begins with "Heaven and earth respond in mutual influence, and the ten-thousand things transform and are born" in the hexagrams of Influence and Duration (which represent the first interaction between the Qian and Kun pair separately posited in the beginning of the first half). Jumping over twenty-eight hexagrams, hexagrams #61 and

#62 are once again symmetrical hexagrams. Again, these two hexagrams are related to each other by inverting the lines. Immediately following, there is once again a pair of hexagrams having to do with fire and water; that is, the hexagrams featuring the mutual complementarity of fire and water, After Completion and Before Completion. Obviously, in the whole of the *YiJing*, fire and water are not only the central pivot; but also, at the very periphery of the book, there is a kind of state of mixture of them, which is a kind of state going beyond what we know in nature. And the symmetrical hexagrams of Central Sincerity and Small Passage (#61 and #62) are a "doorway" opening and closing, affording entrance into this special state, a gateway to heaven, just like the old idea of the ChangHe gate.

(3) We will now investigate this type of condition of blending together fire and water which is radically different from what we know in nature. The hexagrams After Completion and Before Completion have a type of transformational function. If we take the twelve lines which together comprise these two hexagrams, and one by one change each one to its opposite, so that *yin* becomes *yang* or *yang* becomes *yin*, then as a result, the transformed hexagrams that are produced fall only into the following three groups: (a) #49 and #50; (b) #3, #4, #5, and #6; and finally (c) #35, #36, #37, #38, #39, and #40. (Randomly choose any other two pairs and perform the same kind of

operation on them, and the results will not produce the same orderly distribution.) This transformational function's axis of rotation is the most sacred ritual vessel of the bronze age (the Ding tripod hexagram). And its intermediate region accesses a segment of hexagrams at the very beginning of the classic (the hexagrams named: Difficulty at the Beginning, Youthful Folly, Waiting (for Nourishment), and Dispute). Whereas at its peripheral arms, it accesses the center of the classic (the hexagrams named: Progress, Injury of the Light, Family, Opposition, Obstruction, Deliverance). For this reason, the transformational function, this spiral-shaped rotation which issues from the very apex of the *YiJing*, also can be considered to be a kind of refractive condition, which rays down into the base and into the central regions of the *Classic of Change*.

Note: at this point we have already seen enough evidence for us to interpret "water" and "fire" as narrative tools, appropriate to inscribe the pivotal turning-point into the center of a series. For this reason, we can look back to a problem we encountered earlier. In the *Chronicle of Zuo*, the material in the thirtieth year of Kong Qiu especially emphasized the theme of the mutual complementarity of fire and water. The life of Kongzi the Sage is representative; but the question is: representative of what? If ancient society itself already had long since possessed a kind of paradigmatic model, to symbolize the life experience which each individual was to pass through, then later on, wouldn't Kong Qiu follow the same type of guidelines to map out his own manifestation in time? The locus around the thirtieth position in the *YiJing* belongs to fire and water. For this reason, in the *Chronicles of Zuo*, around the thirtieth year of Kongzi's life, someone has posited symbolism of water and fire. We will discuss some other evidence concerning this aspect in a little more detail below.

(4) Besides the examples considered above, the *YiJing* still has quite a good deal of formal evidence which can be used to show its structural organization. Here, because of limitations of space, we can raise only one more kind of illustration. The formal arrangement of the *ZhouYi* can be seen from many different types of symmetrical phenomena. For instance, from hexagram #7 (Army) to #16 (Impulse), this device containing ten hexagrams manifests a sort of perfect symmetry: if the central hexagrams of Peace and Stagnation are taken as the pivotal rotation-point, the rest of the hexagrams to the left and the right of it are mutually inverted realizations of each other (Army and Holding Together hexagrams are the inversions of Fellowship with People and Great Possession hexagrams, just as Small Domestication and Conduct hexagrams are inversions of Modesty and Impulse hexagrams). These rigorously symmetrical relations absolutely could not be random; they certainly have

been deliberately arranged.

Other regions appear in the same way to have had their order arranged. The segment from hexagram #31 to #40 (Xian to Xie) is structurally very similar to the segment from #41 to #50 (Sun to Ding). Especially, the segment beginning from hexagram #43 through to hexagram #50 is a thoroughly integrated arrangement. First, look at these eight hexagrams' "symmetrical trigrams": from hexagram #43 to hexagram #50, there is a very orderly array of all four of the trigrams which remain the same under rotation about the horizontal axis: Qian, Qian, Kun, Kun, Kan, Kan, Li, Li. At the same time, the asymmetrical trigrams which these eight hexagrams display consist of a regular alternation of Dui, Sun, Dui, Sun, Dui, Sun, Dui, Sun. If we further attend to the fact that the head pair of hexagrams for both of these segments of ten (i.e., hexagrams #31 and #32 (Xian and Heng), as well as #41 and #42 (Sun and Yi)) are each inversions of the head pair in the other segment, and consider as well that the distribution of symmetrical and asymmetrical trigrams is quite similar between the two segments, then we can announce with confidence our finding that these two sections have been arranged in parallel.

Looking at it in this way, the existence of a formal arrangement of the *YiJing* ought to be beyond dispute. However, the structure of the *Classic of Changes* is not simply a formal matter (the disposition of lines and hexagrams), but is also a matter of the symbolic content of its textual material, which has also undergone careful arrangement. Its form and its content are incorporated together as one phenomenon. We should say that the *Zhou Yi* is a "cosmological blueprint." It does not simply use written language to expound discursively upon certain philosophical principles; more important, it structurally manifests the cosmological organization of its time. Because of this, the various shapes of the *Classic of Change* (especially its triangular shape) contain the contours and features of its contemporary cosmos. From the distribution of the symbolic network of its written text, we can infer a yearly round of the cycle of the four seasons (Note: of course the methods of calculation popular in the Han Dynasty, such as Hexagram Qi, or Seven Parts, Six Days, etc., also proclaimed this proposition; the distributional investigation presently referred to has a very different basis and different results); we can also infer the three stages of the time of a typical ritual process (just as the JiaoTeSheng chapter of the *LiJi* states: "First perform the ablution, then usher in the sacrifice": in hexagram #20 (Guan) of the *YiJing*, one finds the phrase, "The ablution is made but not yet the offering," after which hexagrams #29 and #30 contain details relevant to sacrifice ("The Pit" is the trench dug before the sacrificial slaughter in order to catch the beasts' blood, while the Li hexagram contains the only instance in the entirety of the *YiJing* of the words, "beheading"); and it is not until hexagram #50 (the Ding tripod) that "the *ding* vessel is full of offerings"). Again, the *Classic of Changes* itself is similarly the model of many aspects of the bases and the functions of the ancient society. If ancient China had age grades to assign different cohorts to different social positions, then the *YiJing* ought to retain traces of them.

Let's take this proposition about age grades as an hypothesis for examining the *Classic of Changes*. Starting from the beginning, with the Qian and Kun hexagrams as father and mother, and going on through Difficulty at the Beginning (Difficult Birth), Youthful Folly, Waiting (for Nourishment), all these hexagrams (when seen as descriptions of the processes of birth) seem to agree well enough with this hypothesis. However, as soon as one encounters hexagram #6 (Dispute), there may be those who wish to say, "Don't tell me that when the child reaches the age of six, he's hit by a lawsuit?" Actually, this type of distributional analysis cannot be refuted with such an objection. The logic of the *YiJing* is multi-purpose and pluralistic. Besides symbolizing the processes of birth and infancy, the same section is concerned with modeling the domain of special prerogatives of the king (such as: to convene courts of law to listen to disputants, plead for rain, carry out divination, participate in royal hunts, establish feudal lords, transmit the heritage of the royal line ("control the family"), contract strategic marriage alliances, etc.) These functions are all distributed along with those of the processes of birth and infancy in the segment of the first ten hexagrams. To understand the symbolism of any detail in the *Classic of Change*, one cannot simply look superficially at one example at a time, but rather must investigate all the relevant distributional data as they apply to the whole book.

In ancient China, men at age 40 were "strong and served in government"; from this age until the time when they retired from military service at age 50, there were ten years in which they most directly were involved in handling the administrative management of the state. As for hexagram #50 in the *YiJing* (Ding) and the symbolism that follows it, we will return to this shortly for a brief introduction. First, let's scan through the hexagrams from #40 to #50 and examine their symbolic array; we will discover that this section has a very dense distribution of themes dealing with the administrative system, such as: issuing the calendar (#49), elite trade items (#41/#42), calculation and accounts-keeping (*sun* and *yi*), irrigation (#47/#48; as well, #43/#44 should be explicated as involving problems of symbolism of agricultural and irrigation practices, etc.). At the same time, the two hexagrams at the center of this segment (#45/#46) also should be able to be explained in terms of a connection with high-level state functions (convening assemblies, ascending platforms, holding certain ceremonies, etc.). These further explanations must be temporarily delayed until the next opportunity to write about them.

Men "marry at 30," from 30 to 40 is the age when men were "robust and had a house": it is the period when men were to set up housekeeping and establish their families. It is just for this reason that in the *Classic of Change*, the "Family" hexagram is located at #37. Also, this segment involves the diurnal cycles of the sun and moon, as well as symbols of domestic culinary industry, but these aspects must remain unexplored for the time being. For now, what should be emphasized is the hexagram which in the *YiJing* is opposed to that of the Family: that is "Opposition." The textual symbolism in hexagram #38 is filled with various dirty, polluting, and inauspicious details, which make us think of the various kinds of intra-family conflict where the combatants' antipathy is like that of fire and water. This sort of oppositional pair is not so different from the one the *Chronicles of Zuo* sets up between years thirty-seven and thirty-eight of the life of Kongzi: inside one's own family is the wife, outside it are the seductive dangers of beautiful women.

Men at the age of 20 must undergo the Capping Ceremony before they accede to adulthood. This fact should be considered from three aspects: first, the Capping Rite is a marker of social distinction; second, its educational significance; and third, the character of ordeal in coming-of-age ceremonies. In ancient and traditional societies, the events in an individual's life which are especially full of meaning, such as coming-of-age and marriage, naturally must resort to a variety of markers to express the new social status. The Capping Rite the men undergo at age 20 have this social function; having passed through it, they could go on to serve in the military and (when they reached the age of 30) to get married. The rite which, for the women, was analogous to this one, was the Pinning Ceremony; only having undergone it (at age 15) could they marry (at age 20). In all of the *YiJing*, the only mention made of anything like a "hairpin" is at hexagram #16 (Impulse), the nine in the fourth place, which says, "You gather friends around you like a hair clasp gathers the hair"; the fact that this symbol is deployed just at this locus is an important piece of evidence for the arrangement of the *Classic of Change* according to what would be relevant to an individual at the age indicated by the number of the hexagram. And the next hexagram (#17, Following) also has several phrases which involve the theme of coming into adulthood, such as: "Bind the child, lose the adult," "Bind the adult, lose the child," etc. As well, the complex psychological state of the adolescent can at times give rise to all sorts of darkness or corruption, such as the situations narrated in the Pollution hexagram (#18). In sum, in the hexagrams around #17, the *YiJing* assembles elements in which there are more than a few points in common with the records at the seventeenth year of Kong Qiu documented in the *Chronicles of Zuo*. This is a situation to which it would be worth devoting a lot more extended consideration.

Maturing to adulthood of course is related to education. From the testimony of the classical literature, we know that the education which men received probably took place in a type of men's house. This kind of building was given quite a variety of different names, such as *xu, xiang, xue, mi, biyong,* and so on. This sort of institution was comparable to men's houses in many other traditional societies. Now, hexagram #20 (Observation (from a) Tower) in the *YiJing* is the graphic image of a tower, and as such it should be entered into the list of men's houses just discussed. To prepare for the Capping Ceremony, the young men would receive education in some isolated setting such as the men's house. The acquisition of this knowledge of course depended upon having a teacher, and the condition to devote oneself to the instruction of a master was to provide tuition payment; at that time, the gifts which functioned as tuition payment were rolls of silk and bundles of dried meat (actually, these prestations also were the gifts which

71

were used in negotiating marriages; in this way we can see how ancient society made initiation, education and marriage all share common symbolic functions). In all the *Classic of Change*, there is no better candidate to represent the bundles of dried meat than hexagram #21 (Biting Through). Its lines of text refer to all sorts of meat, such as skin, gristly meat, dried meat of various kinds, etc. There is no other place in all the *YiJing* that has this sort of textual detail. And in hexagram #22 (Adornment) there is the only reference in the entire *YiJing* to rolls of silk. With this kind of evidence, how can we not recognize that there are indications of the social apparatus of its time?

From a viewpoint which is commonplace in anthropology, most of the coming-of-age rituals in traditional societies perform a symbolic process which expresses the death of the initiate's self belonging to the world of childhood, and the rebirth of the initiate in the world of adults. Because of this, in traditional societies, there is often an initiatory ordeal enacted at the coming-of-age ritual, before the youths are given their new status. In the *YiJing*, there is also a framework for this sort of event, upon which one may base an outline sketch of a type of initiatory drama. Its proceedings can be followed beginning with hexagram #21: the bundles of dried meat, which the lines of the hexagram mention, can be said to have "brought down" the master for instruction; at the same time, this prestation has "brought down" the tiger. This tiger's function is ambivalent: on the one hand, it is through its large open mouth that the initiate will die and be reborn; this is its dangerous side. On the other hand, the tiger will protect that sacred, cleansed site of order, and will exorcise away all the evil, polluting beings; this is its benevolent side. (The tiger in mythologies often has this type of bivalent role in many cultures, including contemporary Chinese religion's Tiger God). The evidence from the *YiJing* is as follows: the nine in the fourth position of the Biting Through hexagram is obviously something to eat being held in the mouth of the tiger ("The commentary on the judgement says: There is something within the corners of the mouth; this is called 'Biting Through'"); when this line changes, it goes to hexagram #27 (The Corners of the Mouth): "The tiger stares about with wild looks, with insatiable craving" (six in the fourth place). This is the threat the tiger poses to the initiate. And its benevolent side is based upon the special relation of the Corners of the Mouth hexagram towards the Pollution hexagram (#18). That is to say: the three hexagrams, Pollution, Biting Through, and the Corners of the Mouth, form a triangle. Pollution and Biting Through hexagrams present a contrastive pair, arranged in opposition on either side of hexagram #20 (Observation (from a) Tower), are to be taken as the base of the triangle; its symbolic opposition can be said to be one of rotten versus dried meat (actually, with more careful examination of this contrast, it would turn out to resemble that of the difference between the Aquatic Creatures Man and the Pemmican Man in the *ZhouLi* passage considered earlier). And at the apex of this triangle, the hexagram Corners of the Mouth maintains special relations with the points, Pollution and Biting Through, which define its left and right sides. We have just seen the nature of the special relation between the Corners of the Mouth and Biting Through hexagrams. The evidence pertaining to the relation between the Corners of the Mouth and Pollution hexagrams is as follows: (1) we know from the classical tradition of the enmity between the tiger and pollution (*gu*); (2) in the *YiJing*, these two hexagrams are the endpoints of a segment of exactly ten hexagrams; (3) in the entirety of the first half of the *YiJing*, hexagrams #17/#18 and #27/#28 are the only hexagrams constituted by two asymmetrical trigrams each. In view of these considerations, we have sufficient reason to say that the designers of the *Classic of Changes* created an holistic framework in order to display the significance of the social function of the coming-of-age initiation. Therefore, when the *Chronicles of Zuo* array the material of the seventeenth and twenty-seventh year of Kong Qiu, complete with the details of his coming to adulthood and his education, it helps us to understand that in the Spring and Autumn period, there were still those who preserved and passed on this sort of custom. As well, it is really reminiscent of the twentieth passage[8] of the *Laozi*, which is the only entry in the entire *DaoDeJing* to make any mention of the "tower" such as "climb the Spring Tower" does. We can no longer ignore the suspicion that is beginning to form, that the classical texts of ancient China are giving us any number of subtle but undeniable clues about what used to have been a kind of universally-shared symbolic system.

Because the *YiJing* provides such a densely integrated model, for the person doing this sort of research, it is the critical element in the data structure. Only by taking advantage of its formal organization, can we understand how the history and structure at the time were dependent upon number for their resolution in an associated whole. Just because the logical system of numbers presents such finely distinguished matrices, they provide the best resource for this kind of project of classifying cosmological categories. In a word, this kind of thinking sees numbers from the very beginning as being real objects. The cosmological structures brought about by these numbers are able to become the basis of all sorts of phenomena in the experience of human beings, and in so doing,

---

[8] Of course this citation refers to the arrangement whereby the "*Dao Jing*" is found before the "*De Jing*." The author of course knows that these numerical chapter headers did not appear until very late.

they move these phenomena a step towards their abstraction. However, it must also be noted that this style of thinking never made the turn away from the natural world; what we just called the process of abstraction always kept within the domain of cosmology. As a result, the goal of this type of culture was to distinguish level after level of phenomena in the cosmology, according to the structures inherent in them. In this way, these arrays of phenomena, level upon level, each could participate in the logical system founded by the numbers. This was so even to the extent that the counting numbers used in calculation were also influenced by this sort of culture; the conceptual space that the number series occupied also furnished opportunities and resources for the classification of the cosmos. Time equally was encompassed in the spatialized features of the numerical network. And within the axes of this sort of space and time, a wide array of aspects of the organization of human life also was capable for the first time of establishing efficacy. Government and other social mechanisms also were able to ramify their functions in dependency upon this sort of structural system. In this type of medium, human experience takes on significance, and the events which individuals live through, as well as the changes which the society undergoes, consist of a structural rationale which is intelligible. These characteristics show the face of ancient China as it was turned towards structure and history.

The *ZhouYi* allows us access to the organization of this numerical system. Before this essay concludes, I want to turn to a final example in order to prove the enormous range of the cosmological system of these ancient classical texts. From what was said above, we know that numbers resemble real objects; each one of them has its own independent qualities and features. Thinking about it in this way, number forty is a very useful number: because 40 (4 X 10) can be taken as four instances of the totality, it has its usefulness in manifesting phenomena such as the four directions of space. It is just for this reason that the pair of hexagrams #39 and #40 of the *Classic of Changes* (Obstruction and Deliverance) is the only place in the whole classic, excepting the Kun hexagram which symbolizes the great earth, where "west, south... east, north"—the names of all four directions—are mentioned together. (Seen in this way, the "obstruction" in hexagram #39's name is to be seen as the same "bending and bowing" word used in the "Great One, God of the East" chapter of the *Nine Songs*, where it says, "The magical shaman comes bending and bowing in splendid clothes..."; and the textual details of this hexagram #39, which use the formula, "Obstruction going out, X coming in..." would be read as the ritual invocation of various species of good fortune (substituting for X in the formula) during the course of rituals driving the threatening pollution outside and towards the four directions. Moreover, hexagram #40's name "Deliverance" (*xie*), besides the commentators' meaning of "release," cannot be kept from having some connection with the domain of dismemberment (*jie*) rites at the four gates.) Since 40 is such a good number, then 50 is an even more useful one; 50 (5 X 10) after all increases the power of 40 by adding a totality to the center point. We already know that in the *YiJing* the hexagram #50 is the Ding tripod; putting the most sacred bronze vessel, and the vessel form the most representative of the ancient traditional culture, into this fiftieth position is an obvious gesture carrying a very significant meaning. Furthermore, the next hexagram following Ding also mentions "sacrificial spoon and chalice," ritual instruments which clearly associate its text with the context of sacrificial offering established by the previous hexagram (we still do not have a very good idea of whatever the "Gen" of the next following hexagram might be; but if it is, as some suggest, to be read as "gnawing," or as the old *Gui Cang* text has it, "wolf," then we could say that hexagram #52 is—so to speak—"waiting" to devour the sacrificial meat offered in the *ding* vessels). The other details arranged from hexagram #50 to #60 in the *YiJing* can for the time being be left undiscussed; but generally, because there are some mentions of "scribes," "shamans" and other indications which are suitable to officers of the royal court (actually, Feng—the name of the central hexagram #55—was one of the more important capital cities of the Western Zhou), if we thus were to suppose that this segment represents the highest level of social status and sacred function, we would find a good deal of evidence to support such a viewpoint.

Since the *Zhou Yi* provides us with such excellent clues, why don't we take the opportunity to explore other examples of the useful organizing power of the number 50? Let's look for indications in the *Chronicles of Zuo* and in the *Lun Yu*. In the *Chronicles of Zuo*, when the narrative gets to the fiftieth year of Kong Qiu, which is the 8th year of Duke Ding, the records of this year include the episode of "Thieves Steal the Precious Jade and Great Bow." The occasion for this scenario to unfold was the "Ritual Di for Duke Xi." In the *Chronicles of Zuo*, this story has a somewhat ridiculous aspect: when things go downhill to this point, clearly they have gotten hopelessly out of control! (And the next year, when Yang Hu returns the stolen jade and bow, the chronicles go into great detail on this occasion to explain the difference between "get" and "obtain," which in fact is a foreshadowing of the usage involved in the "obtaining the unicorn" passage: in other words a foreshadowing of the death of Kongzi.) This section of the documentation is both comical and tragic. The symbol at its center is the ancient and extremely holy Di ceremony.

The fiftieth position in the *YiJing* is the most sacred bronze vessel *ding*, while the narrative of the fiftieth year of the life of Kong Qiu writes about the archaic Di ceremony to pay respects to the high ancestor. What about the *Lun Yu*? If we count passage by passage in the *Lun Yu* until we reach the fiftieth entry (which is 3.10), suddenly there appear in the text two paragraphs concerning the Di ritual. This is the only place in the entirety of the *Lun Yu* where the character "Di" appears at all. How can it be such a coincidence that all these documents use the number 50 to arrange these symbolisms which belong to the highest level of their cultural values?

The reason that the *Chronicles of Zuo* and the *Lun Yu* have this sort of arrangement is in order to express the circumstance that, although the movement of history has brought about the obvious erosion of the Zhou Dynasty, nonetheless basically this culture still existed: to the point that even the symbolic system used to record this debacle of erosion originally belonged to that early period's culture. Although the documentation provided by Kongzi seems, superficially, to be satirizing the regression of the contemporary society, the organization of these materials implies still another, more positive, intent. The parts of the

Chronicles of Zuo pertaining to Kong Qiu, and the *Lun Yu*, all preserve quite a lot of relations with the *ZhouYi*.

Mengzi once wrote: "Kongzi was the sage of temporality" (5B.1). Kong Qiu, in his every action, understood how to coordinate the temporal conditions of these actions. He was able to await the most appropriate occasion before taking the most fitting action. We can also say that Kong Qiu's whole life, as well as the classical texts which he left behind, are also a kind of embodiment of temporality. As far as Kongzi was concerned, his age incorporated a kind of symbolic echo of his own personal existence. Kongzi the Sage could manifest in his own historical time the current paradigm of the exemplary human life. As this essay has brought out, the cosmology that ancient China already had, as well as its cosmological blueprint, the *Classic of Change*, was eminently able to meet the conditions for going on to become the conceptual model for Kongzi's time.